Visit classzone.com and get connected

Online resources for students and parents

ClassZone resources provide instruction, practice, and learning support.

eEdition Plus ONLINE

This interactive version of the text encourages students to explore science.

Content Review Online

Interactive review reinforces the big idea and key concepts of each chapter.

SciLinks

NSTA-selected links provide relevant Web resources correlated to the text.

Chapter-Based Support

Math tutorials, news, resources, test practice, and a misconceptions database help students succeed.

Now it all clicks!™

CLASSZONE.COM

McDougal Littell

Life Over Time

classification

FOSSIL

species

preserved
remains

LIFE SCIENCE

A ▶ Cells and Heredity
B ▶ Life Over Time
C ▶ Diversity of Living Things
D ▶ Ecology
E ▶ Human Biology

EARTH SCIENCE

A ▶ Earth's Surface
B ▶ The Changing Earth
C ▶ Earth's Waters
D ▶ Earth's Atmosphere
E ▶ Space Science

PHYSICAL SCIENCE

A ▶ Matter and Energy
B ▶ Chemical Interactions
C ▶ Motion and Forces
D ▶ Waves, Sound, and Light
E ▶ Electricity and Magnetism

Acknowledgments: Excerpts and adaptations from *National Science Education Standards* by the National Academy of Sciences. Copyright © 1996 by the National Academy of Sciences. Reprinted with permission from the National Academies Press, Washington, D.C.

Excerpts and adaptations from *Benchmarks for Science Literacy: Project 2061.* Copyright © 1993 by the American Association for the Advancement of Science. Reprinted with permission.

ISBN: 0-618-33436-X   3 4 5 6 7 8 VJM 08 07 06 05 04

Internet Web Site: http://www.mcdougallittell.com

Science Consultants

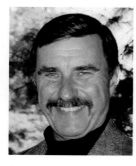

Chief Science Consultant

James Trefil, Ph.D. is the Clarence J. Robinson Professor of Physics at George Mason University. He is the author or co-author of more than 25 books, including *Science Matters* and *The Nature of Science*. Dr. Trefil is a member of the American Association for the Advancement of Science's Committee on the Public Understanding of Science and Technology. He is also a fellow of the World Economic Forum and a frequent contributor to *Smithsonian* magazine.

Rita Ann Calvo, Ph.D. is Senior Lecturer in Molecular Biology and Genetics at Cornell University, where for 12 years she also directed the Cornell Institute for Biology Teachers. Dr. Calvo is the 1999 recipient of the College and University Teaching Award from the National Association of Biology Teachers.

Kenneth Cutler, M.S. is the Education Coordinator for the Julius L. Chambers Biomedical Biotechnology Research Institute at North Carolina Central University. A former middle school and high school science teacher, he received a 1999 Presidential Award for Excellence in Science Teaching.

Instructional Design Consultants

Douglas Carnine, Ph.D. is Professor of Education and Director of the National Center for Improving the Tools of Educators at the University of Oregon. He is the author of seven books and over 100 other scholarly publications, primarily in the areas of instructional design and effective instructional strategies and tools for diverse learners. Dr. Carnine also serves as a member of the National Institute for Literacy Advisory Board.

Linda Carnine, Ph.D. consults with school districts on curriculum development and effective instruction for students struggling academically. A former teacher and school administrator, Dr. Carnine also co-authored a popular remedial reading program.

Donald Steely, Ph.D. serves as principal investigator at the Oregon Center for Applied Science (ORCAS) on federal grants for science and language arts programs. His background also includes teaching and authoring of print and multimedia programs in science, mathematics, history, and spelling.

Sam Miller, Ph.D. is a middle school science teacher and the Teacher Development Liaison for the Eugene, Oregon, Public Schools. He is the author of curricula for teaching science, mathematics, computer skills, and language arts.

Vicky Vachon, Ph.D. consults with school districts throughout the United States and Canada on improving overall academic achievement with a focus on literacy. She is also co-author of a widely used program for remedial readers.

Content Reviewers

John Beaver, Ph.D.
Ecology
Professor, Director of Science Education Center
College of Education and Human Services
Western Illinois University
Macomb, IL

Donald J. DeCoste, Ph.D.
Matter and Energy, Chemical Interactions
Chemistry Instructor
University of Illinois
Urbana-Champaign, IL

Dorothy Ann Fallows, Ph.D., MSc
Diversity of Living Things, Microbiology
Partners in Health
Boston, MA

Michael Foote, Ph.D.
The Changing Earth, Life Over Time
Associate Professor
Department of the Geophysical Sciences
The University of Chicago
Chicago, IL

Lucy Fortson, Ph.D.
Space Science
Director of Astronomy
Adler Planetarium and Astronomy Museum
Chicago, IL

Elizabeth Godrick, Ph.D.
Human Biology
Professor, CAS Biology
Boston University
Boston, MA

Isabelle Sacramento Grilo, M.S.
The Changing Earth
Lecturer, Department of the Geological Sciences
San Diego State University
San Diego, CA

David Harbster, MSc
Diversity of Living Things
Professor of Biology
Paradise Valley Community College
Phoenix, AZ

Richard D. Norris, Ph.D.
Earth's Waters
Professor of Paleobiology
Scripps Institution of Oceanography
University of California, San Diego
La Jolla, CA

Donald B. Peck, M.S.
Motion and Forces; Waves, Sound, and Light;
  Electricity and Magnetism
Director of the Center for Science Education (retired)
Fairleigh Dickinson University
Madison, NJ

Javier Penalosa, Ph.D.
Diversity of Living Things, Plants
Associate Professor, Biology Department
Buffalo State College
Buffalo, NY

Raymond T. Pierrehumbert, Ph.D.
Earth's Atmosphere
Professor in Geophysical Sciences (Atmospheric Science)
The University of Chicago
Chicago, IL

Brian J. Skinner, Ph.D.
Earth's Surface
Eugene Higgins Professor of Geology and Geophysics
Yale University
New Haven, CT

Nancy E. Spaulding, M.S.
Earth's Surface, The Changing Earth, Earth's Waters
Earth Science Teacher (retired)
Elmira Free Academy
Elmira, NY

Steven S. Zumdahl, Ph.D.
Matter and Energy, Chemical Interactions
Professor Emeritus of Chemistry
University of Illinois
Urbana-Champaign, IL

Susan L. Zumdahl, M.S.
Matter and Energy, Chemical Interactions
Chemistry Education Specialist
University of Illinois
Urbana-Champaign, IL

Safety Consultant

Juliana Texley, Ph.D.
Former K–12 Science Teacher and School Superintendent
Boca Raton, FL

English Language Advisor

Judy Lewis, M.A.
Director, State and Federal Programs for reading proficiency
and high risk populations
Rancho Cordova, CA

Teacher Panel Members

Carol Arbour
Tallmadge Middle School,
Tallmadge, OH

Patty Belcher
Goodrich Middle School,
Akron, OH

Gwen Broestl
Luis Munoz Marin Middle School,
Cleveland, OH

Al Brofman
Tehipite Middle School,
Fresno, CA

John Cockrell
Clinton Middle School,
Columbus, OH

Jenifer Cox
Sylvan Middle School,
Citrus Heights, CA

Linda Culpepper
Martin Middle School,
Charlotte, NC

Kathleen Ann DeMatteo
Margate Middle School,
Margate, FL

Melvin Figueroa
New River Middle School,
Ft. Lauderdale, FL

Doretha Grier
Kannapolis Middle School,
Kannapolis, NC

Robert Hood
Alexander Hamilton Middle School,
Cleveland, OH

Scott Hudson
Covedale Elementary School,
Cincinnati, OH

Loretta Langdon
Princeton Middle School,
Princeton, NC

Carlyn Little
Glades Middle School,
Miami, FL

Ann Marie Lynn
Amelia Earhart Middle School,
Riverside, CA

James Minogue
Lowe's Grove Middle School,
Durham, NC

Joann Myers
Buchanan Middle School,
Tampa, FL

Barbara Newell
Charles Evans Hughes Middle School,
Long Beach, CA

Anita Parker
Kannapolis Middle School,
Kannapolis, NC

Greg Pirolo
Golden Valley Middle School,
San Bernardino, CA

Laura Pottmyer
Apex Middle School,
Apex, NC

Lynn Prichard
Booker T. Washington Middle Magnet
School, Tampa, FL

Jacque Quick
Walter Williams High School,
Burlington, NC

Robert Glenn Reynolds
Hillman Middle School,
Youngstown, OH

Stacy Rinehart
Lufkin Road Middle School,
Apex, NC

Theresa Short
Abbott Middle School,
Fayetteville, NC

Rita Slivka
Alexander Hamilton Middle School,
Cleveland, OH

Marie Sofsak
B F Stanton Middle School,
Alliance, OH

Nancy Stubbs
Sweetwater Union Unified School District,
Chula Vista, CA

Sharon Stull
Quail Hollow Middle School,
Charlotte, NC

Donna Taylor
Okeeheelee Middle School,
West Palm Beach, FL

Sandi Thompson
Harding Middle School,
Lakewood, OH

Lori Walker
Audubon Middle School & Magnet Center,
Los Angeles, CA

Teacher Lab Evaluators

Andrew Boy
W.E.B. DuBois Academy,
Cincinnati, OH

Jill Brimm-Byrne
Albany Park Academy,
Chicago, IL

Gwen Broestl
Luis Munoz Marin Middle School,
Cleveland, OH

Al Brofman
Tehipite Middle School,
Fresno, CA

Michael A. Burstein
The Rashi School,
Newton, MA

Trudi Coutts
Madison Middle School,
Naperville, IL

Jenifer Cox
Sylvan Middle School,
Citrus Heights, CA

Larry Cwik
Madison Middle School,
Naperville, IL

Jennifer Donatelli
Kennedy Junior High School,
Lisle, IL

Melissa Dupree
Lakeside Middle School,
Evans, GA

Carl Fechko
Luis Munoz Marin Middle School,
Cleveland, OH

Paige Fullhart
Highland Middle School,
Libertyville, IL

Sue Hood
Glen Crest Middle School,
Glen Ellyn, IL

William Luzader
Plymouth Community Intermediate School,
Plymouth, MA

Ann Min
Beardsley Middle School,
Crystal Lake, IL

Aileen Mueller
Kennedy Junior High School,
Lisle, IL

Nancy Nega
Churchville Middle School,
Elmhurst, IL

Oscar Newman
Sumner Math and Science Academy,
Chicago, IL

Lynn Prichard
Booker T. Washington Middle Magnet
School, Tampa, FL

Jacque Quick
Walter Williams High School,
Burlington, NC

Stacy Rinehart
Lufkin Road Middle School,
Apex, NC

Seth Robey
Gwendolyn Brooks Middle School,
Oak Park, IL

Kevin Steele
Grissom Middle School,
Tinley Park, IL

McDougal Littell Science

Life Over Time

eEdition

Life Over Time

Unit Features

SCIENTIFIC AMERICAN

1 The History of Life on Earth   6

the **BIG** idea

Living things, like Earth itself, change over time.

*How do scientists learn about the
history of life on Earth?* page 6

How many different types of organisms do you see and how would you group them? page 40

Features

Visual Highlights

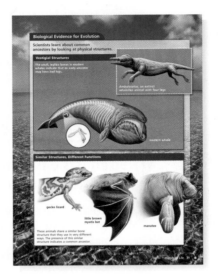

Internet Resources @ ClassZone.com

INVESTIGATIONS AND ACTIVITIES

EXPLORE THE BIG IDEA

Chapter Opening Inquiries

CHAPTER INVESTIGATION

Full-Period Labs

EXPLORE

Introductory Inquiry Activities

INVESTIGATE

Skill Labs

Standards and Benchmarks

Each chapter in **Life Over Time** covers some of the learning goals that are described in the *National Science Education Standards* (NSES) and the Project 2061 *Benchmarks for Science Literacy.* Selected content and skill standards are shown below in shortened form. The following National Science Education Standards are covered on pages xii-xxvii, in Frontiers in Science, and in Timelines in Science, as well as in chapter features and laboratory investigations: Understandings About Scientific Inquiry (A.9), Science and Technology in Society (F.5), Understandings About Science and Technology (E.6), and Science as a Human Endeavor (G.1), Nature of Science (G.2), History of Science (G.3).

Content Standards

1 History of Life

National Science Education Standards

C.1.b	Most organisms are single cells; other organisms are multicellular.
C.5.a	Relationships among organisms can be found by looking at internal structures, chemical processes, and the evidence of common ancestry.
C.5.b	Biological evolution has led to greater species diversity over time.
C.5.c	Species may become extinct if they cannot survive changes in the environment.
D.2.b	Fossils provide evidence of how life and the environment have changed.

Project 2061 Benchmarks

5.B.3	New varieties of species have resulted from selective breeding.
5.F.1	Small differences between parents and offspring can accumulate over time so that descendants are very different from their ancestors.
5.F.2	Individual organisms with certain traits are more likely than others to survive and have offspring.

2 Classification of Living Things

National Science Education Standards

C.2.e	The characteristics of an organism can be described in terms of a combination of traits.
C.5.a	Millions of species of animals, plants, and microorganisms are alive today.
G.2.a	Scientists change their ideas about nature when they find new experimental evidence that does not match their existing explanations.

Project 2061 Benchmarks

5.A.3	In classifying organisms, biologists consider the internal and external structures.
5.A.2	Animals and plants have a great variety of body plans that contributes to their being able to make or find food and reproduce.

3 Population Dynamics

National Science Education Standards

F.2.b	Causes of environmental degradation and resource depletion vary.
F.2.a	When an area becomes overpopulated, the environment will become degraded.
C.4.a	A population consists of all individuals of a species that occur together at a given place and time.
C.4.d	Resources and other factors can limit population growth.

Project 2061 Benchmarks

4.B.8	Water can be polluted, becoming unsuitable for life, or it can be depleted.
4.C.7	Some human activities have decreased Earth's capacity to support life.
5.D.1	In all environments, organisms with similar needs may compete for resources.

Process and Skills Standards

National Science Education Standards

A.1	Identify questions that can be answered through scientific methods.
A.2	Design and conduct a scientific investigation.
A.3	Use appropriate tools and techniques to gather and analyze data.
A.4	Use evidence to describe, predict, explain, and model.
A.5	Think critically to find relationships between results and interpretations.
A.6	Give alternative explanations and predictions.
A.7	Communicate procedures, results, and conclusions.
A.8	Use mathematics in all aspects of scientific inquiry.

Project 2061 Benchmarks

9.A.2	Use a number line to extend on the other side of zero to represent things—such as time—that can be measured on either side of some reference point.
9.B.2	Use mathematics to describe change.
9.C.6	Choose an appropriate scale for displaying information.
9.D.3	Use information about the mean, median, and mode of a data set appropriately.
9.D.5	Use a large, well-chosen sample to accurately represent the whole. Many ways of choosing a sample can make it unrepresentative of the whole.

11.B.1	Use models to think about processes.
11.D.2	With complex systems, use summaries, averages, ranges, and examples.
12.A.1	Know why it is important in science to keep honest, clear, and accurate records.
12.A.2	Investigate, using hypotheses.
12.A.3	See multiple ways to interpret the same results.
12.C.3	Use appropriate units, use and read instruments that measure length, volume, weight, time, rate, and temperature.
12.D.1	Use tables and graphs to organize information and identify relationships.
12.D.2	Read, interpret, and describe tables and graphs.
12.D.3	Locate information in reference books and other resources.
12.D.4	Understand different types of charts and graphs, including circle charts, bar graphs, line graphs, data tables, diagrams, and symbols.

Introducing Life Science

Scientists are curious. Since ancient times, they have been asking and answering questions about the world around them. Scientists are also very suspicious of the answers they get. They carefully collect evidence and test their answers many times before accepting an idea as correct.

In this book you will see how scientific knowledge keeps growing and changing as scientists ask new questions and rethink what was known before. The following sections will help get you started.

What Is Life Science?

Life science is the study of living things. As you study life science, you will observe and read about a variety of organisms, from huge redwood trees to the tiny bacteria that cause sore throats. Because Earth is home to such a great variety of living things, the study of life science is rich and exciting.

But life science doesn't simply include learning the names of millions of organisms. It includes big ideas that help us to understand how all these living things interact with their environment. Life science is the study of characteristics and needs that all living things have in common. It's also a study of changes—both daily changes as well as changes that take place over millions of years. Probably most important, in studying life science, you will explore the many ways that all living things—including you—depend upon Earth and its resources.

The text and visuals in this book will invite you into the world of living things and provide you with the key concepts you'll need in your study. Activities offer a chance for you to investigate some aspects of life science on your own. The four unifying principles listed below provide a way for you to connect the information and ideas in this program.

- **All living things share common characteristics.**

- **All living things share common needs.**

- **Living things meet their needs through interactions with the environment.**

- **The types and numbers of living things change over time.**

the **BIG** idea

Each chapter begins with a big idea. Keep in mind that each big idea relates to one or more of the unifying principles.

All living things share common characteristics.

Birds nest among the plants of a reed marsh as sunlight shines and a breeze blows. Which of these is alive? Warblers and plants are living things, but sunlight and breezes are not. All living things share common characteristics that distinguish them from nonliving things.

What It Means

This unifying principle helps you explore one of the biggest questions in science, "What is life?" Let's take a look at four characteristics that distinguish living things from nonliving things: organization, growth, reproduction, and response.

Organization

If you stand a short distance from a reed warbler's nest, you can observe the largest level of organization in a living thing—the **organism** itself. Each bird is an organism. If you look at a leaf under a microscope, you can observe the smallest level of organization capable of performing all the activities of life, a **cell.** All living things are made of cells.

Growth

Most living things grow and develop. Growth often involves not only an increase in size, but also an increase in complexity, such as a tadpole growing into a frog. If all goes well, the small warblers in the picture will grow to the size of their parent.

Reproduction

Most living things produce offspring like themselves. Those offspring are also able to reproduce. That means that reed warblers produce reed warblers, which in turn produce more reed warblers.

Response

You've probably noticed that your body adjusts to changes in your surroundings. If you are exploring outside on a hot day, you may notice that you sweat. On a cold day, you may shiver. Sweating and shivering are examples of response.

Why It's Important

People of all ages experience the urge to explore and understand the living world. Understanding the characteristics of living things is a good way to start this exploration of life. In addition, knowing about the characteristics of living things helps you identify

- similarities and differences among various organisms
- key questions to ask about any organism you study

All living things share common needs.

What do you need to stay alive? What does an animal like a fish or a coral need to stay alive? All living things have common needs.

What It Means

Inside every living thing, chemical reactions constantly change materials into new materials. For these reactions to occur, an organism needs energy, water and other materials, and living space.

Energy

You use energy all the time. Movement, growth, and sleep all require energy, which you get from food. Plants use the energy of sunlight to make sugar for energy. Almost all animals get their energy by eating either plants or other animals that eat plants.

Water and Other Materials

Water is an important material in the cells of all living things. The chemical reactions inside cells take place in water, and water plays a part in moving materials around within organisms.

Other materials are also essential for life. For example, plants must have carbon dioxide from the air to make sugar. Plants and animals both use oxygen to release the energy stored in sugar. You and other animals that live on land get oxygen when you breathe in air. The fish swimming around the coral reef in the picture have gills, which allow them to get oxygen that is dissolved in the water.

Living Space

You can think of living space as a home—a space that protects you from external conditions and a place where you can get materials such as water and air. The ocean provides living space for the coral that makes up this coral reef. The coral itself provides living space for many other organisms.

Why It's Important

Understanding the needs of living things helps people make wise decisions about resources. This knowledge can also help you think carefully about

- the different ways in which various organisms meet their needs for energy and materials
- the effects of adding chemicals to the water and air around us
- the reasons why some types of plants or animals may disappear from an area

Living things meet their needs through interactions with the environment.

A moose chomps on the leaves of a plant. This ordinary event involves many interactions among living and nonliving things within the forest.

What It Means

To understand this unifying principle, take a closer look at the words *environment* and *interactions*.

Environment

The **environment** is everything that surrounds a living thing. An environment is made up of both living and nonliving factors. For example, the environment in this forest includes rainfall, rocks, and soil as well as the moose, the evergreen trees, and the birch trees. In fact, the soil in these forests is called "moose and spruce" soil because it contains materials provided by the animals and evergreens in the area.

Interaction

All living things in an environment meet their needs through interactions. An **interaction** occurs when two or more things act in ways that affect one another. For example, trees and other forest plants can meet their need for energy and materials through interactions with materials in soil and with air and light from the Sun. New plants get living space as birds, wind, and other factors carry seeds from one location to another.

Animals like this moose meet their need for food through interactions with other living things. The moose gets food by eating leaves off trees and other plants. In turn, the moose becomes food for wolves.

Why It's Important

Learning about living things and their environment helps scientists and decision makers address issues such as

- predicting how a change in the moose population would affect the soil in the forest
- determining the ways in which animals harm or benefit the trees in a forest
- developing land for human use without damaging the environment

The types and numbers of living things change over time.

The story of life on Earth is a story of changes. Some changes take place over millions of years. At one time, animals similar to modern fish swam in the area where this lizard now runs.

What It Means

To understand how living things change over time, let's look closely at the terms *diversity* and *adaptation.*

Diversity

You are surrounded by an astonishing variety of living things. This variety is called **biodiversity.** Today, scientists have described and named 1.4 million species. There are even more species that haven't been named. Scientists use the term *species* to describe a group of closely related living things. Members of a **species** are so similar that they can produce offspring that are able to reproduce. Lizards, such as the one you see in the photograph, are so diverse that they make up many different species.

Over the millions of years that life has existed on Earth, new species have originated and others have disappeared. The disappearance of a species is called **extinction.** Fossils, like the one in the photograph, provide evidence of some of the organisms that lived millions of years ago.

Adaptation

Scientists use the term **adaptation** to mean a characteristic of a species that allows members of that species to survive in a particular environment. Adaptations are related to needs. A lizard's legs are an adaptation that allows it to move on land.

Over time, species either develop adaptations to changing environments or they become extinct. The history of living things on Earth is related to the history of the changing Earth. The presence of a fishlike fossil indicates that the area shown in this photograph was once covered by water.

Why It's Important

By learning how living things change over time, you will gain a better understanding of the life that surrounds you and how it survives. Discovering more about the history of life helps scientists to

- identify patterns of relationships among various species
- predict how changes in the environment may affect species in the future

The Nature of Science

You may think of science as a body of knowledge or a collection of facts. More important, however, science is an active process that involves certain ways of looking at the world.

Scientific Habits of Mind

Scientists are curious. They are always asking questions. A scientist who observes that the number of plants in a forest preserve has decreased might ask questions such as, "Are more animals eating the plants?" or "Has the way the land is used affected the numbers of plants?" Scientists around the world investigate these and other important questions.

Scientists are observant. They are always looking closely at the world around them. A scientist who studies plants often sees details such as the height of a plant, its flowers, and how many plants live in a particular area.

Scientists are creative. They draw on what they know to form a possible explanation for a pattern, an event, or a behavior that they have observed. Then scientists create a plan for testing their ideas.

Scientists are skeptical. Scientists don't accept an explanation or answer unless it is based on evidence and logical reasoning. They continually question their own conclusions as well as conclusions suggested by other scientists. Scientists trust only evidence that is confirmed by other people or methods.

A white-tailed deer feeds on many plants, including the trillium shown here.

By measuring the growth of this tree, a scientist can study interactions in the ecosystem.

Science Processes at Work

You can think of science as a continuous cycle of asking and seeking answers to questions about the world. Although there are many processes that scientists use, scientists typically do each of the following:

- Observe and ask a question
- Determine what is known
- Investigate
- Interpret results
- Share results

Observe and Ask a Question

It may surprise you that asking questions is an important skill.
A scientific investigation may start when a scientist asks a question.
Perhaps scientists observe an event or a process that they don't understand, or perhaps answering one question leads to another.

Determine What Is Known

When beginning an inquiry, scientists find out what is already known about a question. They study results from other scientific investigations, read journals, and talk with other scientists. A biologist who is trying to understand how the change in the number of deer in an area affects plants will study reports of censuses taken for both plants and animals.

Investigate

Investigating is the process of collecting evidence. Two important ways of collecting evidence are observing and experimenting.

Observing is the act of noting and recording an event, a characteristic, a behavior, or anything else detected with an instrument or with the senses. For example, a scientist notices that plants in one part of the forest are not thriving. She sees broken plants and compares the height of the plants in one area with the height of those in another.

An **experiment** is an organized procedure during which all factors but the one being studied are controlled. For example, the scientist thinks the reason some plants in the forest are not thriving may be that deer are eating the flowers off the plants. An experiment she might try is to mark two similar parts of an area where the plants grow and then build a fence around one part so the deer can't get to the plants there. The fence must be constructed so the same amounts of light, air, and water reach the plants. The only factor that changes is contact between plants and the deer.

Close observation of the Colorado potato beetle led scientists to a biological pesticide that can help farmers control this insect pest.

Forming hypotheses and making predictions are two other skills involved in scientific investigations. A **hypothesis** is a tentative explanation for an observation or a scientific problem that can be tested by further investigation. For example, since at least 1900, Colorado potato beetles were known to be resistant to chemical insecticides. Yet the numbers of beetles were not as large as expected. It was hypothesized that bacteria living in the beetles' environment were killing many beetles. A **prediction** is an expectation of what will be observed or what will happen and can be used to test a hypothesis. It was predicted that certain bacteria would kill Colorado potato beetles. This prediction was confirmed when a bacterium called *Bt* was discovered to kill Colorado potato beetles and other insect pests.

Interpret Results

As scientists investigate, they analyze their evidence, or data, and begin to draw conclusions. **Analyzing data** involves looking at the evidence gathered through observations or experiments and trying to identify any patterns that might exist in the data. Often scientists need to make additional observations or perform more experiments before they are sure of their conclusions. Many times scientists make new predictions or revise their hypotheses.

Computers help scientists analyze the sequence of base pairs in the DNA molecule.

Share Results

An important part of scientific investigation is sharing results of experiments. Scientists read and publish in journals and attend conferences to communicate with other scientists around the world. Sharing data and procedures gives them a way to test one another's results. They also share results with the public through newspapers, television, and other media.

Living things contain complex molecules such as RNA and DNA. To study them, scientists often use models like the one shown here.

The Nature of Technology

Imagine what life would be like without cars, computers, and cell phones. Imagine having no refrigerator or radio. It's difficult to think of a world without these items we call technology. Technology, however, is more than just machines that make our daily activities easier. Like science, technology is also a process. The process of technology uses scientific knowledge to design solutions to real-world problems.

Science and Technology

Science and technology go hand in hand. Each depends upon the other. Even designing a device as simple as a toaster requires knowledge of how heat flows and which materials are the best conductors of heat. Scientists also use a number of devices to help them collect data. Microscopes, telescopes, spectrographs, and computers are just a few of the tools that help scientists learn more about the world. The more information these tools provide, the more devices can be developed to aid scientific research and to improve modern lives.

The Process of Technological Design

Heart disease is among the leading causes of death today. Doctors have successfully replaced damaged hearts with hearts from donors. Medical engineers have developed pacemakers that improve the ability of a damaged heart to pump blood. But none of these solutions is perfect. Although it is very complex, the heart is really a pump for blood; thus, using technology to build a better replacement pump should be possible. The process of technological design involves many choices. In the case of an artificial heart, choices about how and what to develop involve cost, safety, and patient preference. What kind of technology will result in the best quality of life for the patient?

Identify a Need

Developers of technology must first establish exactly what needs their technology must meet. A healthy heart pumps blood at the rate of 5–30 liters per minute. What type of artificial pump could achieve such rates, responding to changes in activity level? Could such a pump be small enough to implant into a person? How would such a heart be powered? What materials would not be rejected by the human body?

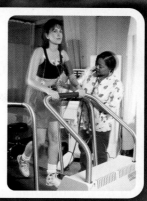

Design and Develop

Several designs for artificial hearts have been proposed. The Jarvik-7 was the first intended to be a long-term replacement for a human heart. The Jarvik-7 did not work very well. Although it lengthened the lives of some patients, their quality of life was poor. Doctors and engineers knew they needed to refine the design further. For example, the heart needed to be smaller, and it needed to have a better power system. The heart also needed to be made out of a better material so that it would not cause blood clots when implanted into a patient.

Test and Improve

The new AbioCor heart may hold the solutions to many of these problems. This fully self-contained implantable device makes the goal of replacing a damaged heart seem not so far away. Still, many improvements will be needed before the AbioCor is routinely put into human beings. Tests of the AbioCor are still in progress.

Using McDougal Littell Science

Reading Text and Visuals

This book is organized to help you learn. Use these boxed pointers as a path to help you learn and remember the **Big Ideas** and **Key Concepts**.

Take notes.

Use the strategies on the **Getting Ready to Learn** page.

Read the Big Idea.

As you read **Key Concepts** for the chapter, relate them to **the Big Idea.**

CHAPTER
2
Classifi...
Living

the **BIG** idea

Scientists have developed a system for classifying the great diversity of living things.

Key Concepts

SECTION 2.1 Scientists develop systems for classifying living things.
Learn about why scientists classify living things and about taxonomy.

SECTION 2.2 Biologists use seven levels of classification.
Learn about scientific names, how to classify organisms in seven levels, and dichotomous keys.

SECTION 2.3 Classification systems change as scientists learn more.
Learn how classification systems have changed based on features of cells.

Internet Preview

CLASSZONE.COM
Chapter 2 online resources:
Content Review, Simulation,
4 Resource Centers, Math
Tutorial, Test Practice

B 40 Unit: Life Over Time

CHAPTER 2
Getting Ready to Learn

CONCEPT REVIEW

- Species change over time.
- Fossils and other evidence show that species change.
- New species develop from ancestral species.

VOCABULARY REVIEW

fossil record p. 11
evolution p. 17
ancestor p. 29

See Glossary for definitions.
species, trait, DNA

CONTENT REVIEW
CLASSZONE.COM
Review concepts and vocabulary.

TAKING NOTES

SUPPORTING MAIN IDEAS

Make a chart to show main ideas and the information that supports them. Copy each blue heading. Below each heading, add supporting information, such as reasons, explanations, and examples.

VOCABULARY STRATEGY

Place each vocabulary term at the center of a **description wheel** diagram. Write some words describing it on the spokes.

See the Note-Taking Handbook on pages R45–R51.

B 42 Unit: Life Over Time

SCIENCE NOTEBOOK

Scientists classify millions of species.

Taxonomy is the science of classifying naming organisms.

Classification is the process of arrangi... organisms in groups.

To classify organisms, scientists compa... their characteristics.

organisms
seven levels
arrange into groups
CLASSIFICATION
Linnaeus
Similar trait
systems can change

KEY CONCEPT

2.1 Scientists develop systems for classifying living things.

BEFORE, you learned

- Natural selection helps explain how new species develop
- Evidence indicates that species change over time
- New species develop from ancestral species

NOW, you will learn

- Why scientists classify living things
- That taxonomists study biological relationships
- About evidence used to classify organisms

VOCABULARY

classification p. 44
taxonomy p. 44

THINK ABOUT

How are these organisms similar?

Both a worm and a caterpillar share many characteristics. Both have long, skinny bodies that are divided into segments. But an earthworm moves underground, has no legs or eyes, and can grow back segments that are lost. A caterpillar crawls aboveground and is just one part of a butterfly's life cycle. As you read this chapter, think about whether you would classify these animals together or separately.

Scientists classify millions of species.

About 400 years ago, scientists who studied insects classified them based upon their appearance and behavior. If animals looked alike, researchers concluded that they were related. In the last few centuries scientists have realized that appearances can suggest false connections. Although caterpillars look like worms, they are more like butterflies. In fact, the caterpillar is a stage of a butterfly's life.

For some people, the world seemed to grow larger during the 1600s. Travelers sailed to distant lands and oceans. Scientists went on many of these trips, observing and collecting samples of living things they had never seen before. In addition, the microscope allowed scientists to see tiny organisms that had been invisible before. But how could scientists organize and talk about this wonderful new knowledge?

Chapter 2: **Classification of Living Things** 43 **B**

Reading Text and Visuals

Multicellular Organisms

Around 1.2 billion years ago organisms made up of many cells began to live in Earth's oceans. **Multicellular organisms** are living things made up of many cells. Individual cells within multicellular organisms often perform specific tasks. For example, some cells may capture energy. Other cells might store materials. Still others might carry materials from one part of the organism to another. The most complex species of multicellular organisms have cells that are organized into tissues, organs, and systems.

Recall that all organisms have similar needs for energy, water, materials, and living space. For almost 3 billion years, these needs were met only in oceans. According to fossil records, the earliest multicellular organisms were tiny seaweeds. The earliest animals were similar to today's jellyfish.

CHECK YOUR READING Explain how unicellular and multicellular organisms differ.

Scientists learn about early life by studying different layers of rock

> **Read one paragraph at a time.**
>
> Look for a topic sentence that explains the main idea of the paragraph. Figure out how the details relate to that idea. One paragraph might have several important ideas; you may have to reread to understand.

> **Answer the questions.**
>
> **Check Your Reading** questions will help you remember what you read.

Life on Land

Consider the importance of water. You use it to meet many different needs. Without it, your life would be very different. This is also true for other living things. About 500 million years ago, the first multicellular organisms moved from water to land.

37 million years ago A volcano covers Colorado in a layer of hot ash, smothering plant and animal life for miles.

16,000 years ago The plains look similar to what we see today—except that camels and mammoths roam the area.

Present day Buildings and highways cover the land. Humans have the technology to dig through layers of rock and reconstruct the past.

> **Study the visuals.**
>
> - Read the title.
> - Read all labels and captions.
> - Figure out what the picture is showing. Notice the information in the captions.

Chapter 1: **History of Life** 13 **B**

Doing Labs

To understand science, you have to see it in action. Doing labs helps you understand how things really work.

① Read the entire lab first.

② Follow the procedure.

③ Record the data.

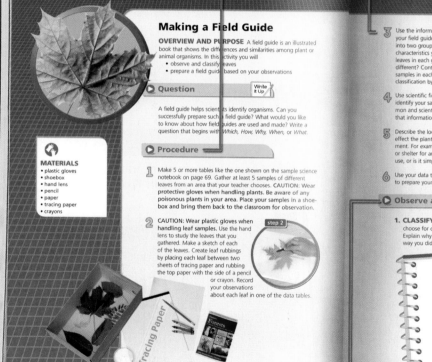

CHAPTER INVESTIGATION

Making a Field Guide

OVERVIEW AND PURPOSE A field guide is an illustrated book that shows the differences and similarities among plant or animal organisms. In this activity you will
• observe and classify leaves
• prepare a field guide based on your observations

▶ Question
Write It Up

A field guide helps scientists identify organisms. Can you successfully prepare such a field guide? What would you like to know about how field guides are used and made? Write a question that begins with *Which, How, Why, When,* or *What.*

▶ Procedure

MATERIALS
• plastic gloves
• shoebox
• hand lens
• pencil
• paper
• tracing paper
• crayons

1. Make 5 or more tables like the one shown on the sample science notebook on page 69. Gather at least 5 samples of different leaves from an area that your teacher chooses. CAUTION: Wear protective gloves when handling plants. Be aware of any poisonous plants in your area. Place your samples in a shoebox and bring them back to the classroom for observation.

2. CAUTION: Wear plastic gloves when handling leaf samples. Use the hand lens to study the leaves that you gathered. Make a sketch of each of the leaves. Create leaf rubbings by placing each leaf between two sheets of tracing paper and rubbing the top paper with the side of a pencil or crayon. Record your observations about each leaf in one of the data tables.

step 2

3. Use the information in your table to prepare your field guide. Start by dividing your leaves into two groups on the basis of one of the characteristics you observed. Then compare the leaves in each group. How are they similar or different? Continue to observe and divide the samples in each group until each leaf is in a classification by itself.

4. Use scientific field guides or other sources to identify your sample leaves. Find out the common and scientific name for each leaf and add that information to your table.

5. Describe the location of each sample and what effect the plant it represents has on its environment. For example, does the plant provide food or shelter for animals? Does it have a commercial use, or is it simply a common weed?

6. Use your data tables, sketches, and leaf rubbings to prepare your field guide for the chosen area.

▶ Observe and Analyze
Write It Up

1. **CLASSIFY** What characteristics did you choose for classifying your leaf samples? Explain why you grouped the leaves the way you did.

2. **ANALYZE** Which characteristics of the leaves you gathered were most useful in finding their scientific names and in identifying them?

▶ Conclude
Write It Up

1. **INFER** Could you use the same characteristics you used to group your samples to classify leaves of other species?

2. **LIMITATIONS** Were there any leaves you could not classify? What would help you classify them?

3. **APPLY** How are field guides useful to scientists working on environmental studies? How are field guides useful to tourists or others who are exploring an environment?

▶ INVESTIGATE Further

CHALLENGE Combine your field guide with those made by all the other members of your class to make one large field guide. Use all the sketches and observations to classify leaves into several large groups.

Making a Field Guide: Leaf 1

Characteristic	Observations
Simple leaf or several leaflets	
Number of lobes	
Texture	
Leaf edge	
Vein patterns	

Common name _____

Scientific name _____

Location where found _____

Uses/role in environment _____

④ Analyze your results.

⑤ Write your lab report.

Using Technology

The Internet is a great source of information about up-to-date science. The ClassZone Web site and NSTA SciLinks have exciting sites for you to explore. Video clips and simulations can make science come alive.

Look for red banners.

Go to **ClassZone.com** to see simulations, visualizations, resource centers, and content review.

Watch the video.

See science at work in the **Scientific American Frontiers** video.

Look up SciLinks.

Go to **scilinks.org** to explore the topic.

The Fossil Record **Code: MDL036**

Life Over Time
Contents Overview

Life By Degrees

What happens when Earth's climate changes? Scientists are studying how climate change has influenced the evolution of life on Earth.

SCIENTIFIC AMERICAN FRONTIERS

Learn about how climate change affected life on Earth. See the video "Noah's Snowball."

Climate and Life

Throughout its history, Earth's climate has changed many times. Often the changes are gradual. They may seem small. However, an average global temperature change of just a few degrees can have a large impact on climate. Small changes in climate then cause big changes for plants and animals.

Before there were humans to record events, Earth recorded its changes in its rocks and fossils. For example, scientists get a sense for Earth's climate at different times in the distant past by looking at fossils, the remains and traces of living things. If scientists find fossils of tropical plants in places near the arctic circle, then they may conclude that the climate in those places was different in the past.

Scientists have found that warmer climates lead to a greater diversity of organisms. One researcher examined fossils of tiny organisms called phytoplankton (FY-toh-PLANK-tuhn). During cooler climate periods, there were fewer types of phytoplankton than during warmer periods. The same is true for other organisms. Peter Wilf and Conrad Labandeira studied fossil plants. They were especially interested in the marks they found on the plants. The marks were left by plant-eating animals who bit the leaves. The warmer the climate was, the more types of plants there were—and the more kinds of animals were eating the plants.

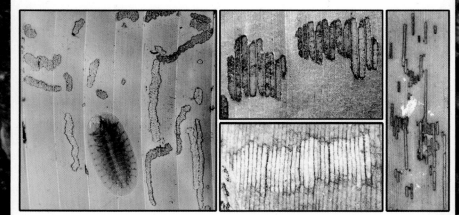

SOURCE: Images © 2000 AAAS

The chew marks of the hispine beetle larva on living ginger in Panama (left) look similar to fossilized chew marks found in Wyoming (three photos right).

Before and after photographs of the sky show that distinct bands appeared due to dust and ash from the 1991 volcanic eruption of Mt. Pinatubo.

Mass Extinction

Several times in Earth's past, many kinds of animals and plants have disappeared in a relatively short time. These events are called mass extinctions. While we don't know for sure what causes them, most scientists think climate change plays a role in mass extinctions.

The largest mass extinction in Earth's history happened at the end of the Permian (PER-mee-uhn) Period about 248 million years ago. Scientists estimate that 90–95 percent of animal species that lived in the water died out. About three quarters of the vertebrates, or animals with backbones, living on land died out too.

Turn of Events

What caused this extinction? Using fossils, scientists have concluded that Earth's climate became cooler. Material from erupting volcanoes may have blocked sunlight long enough to cool the Earth. The cool temperatures and lack of sunlight may have killed plants and animals.

Scientist Peter Ward has been studying the Permian extinction. He looked at ancient African rivers and found evidence that rivers had became clogged with soil. Plants normally holding soil in place may have been wiped out, causing the soil on the riverbanks to loosen. The plant extinction would also have led to animal extinction.

SCIENTIFIC AMERICAN FRONTIERS

View the "Noah's Snowball" segment of your Scientific American Frontiers video to learn about another theory of how climate change affected life on Earth.

IN THIS SCENE FROM THE VIDEO ▶
Fossil hunters examine evidence of early life in China.

DEEP FREEZE Can you imagine what Earth would be like if it were completely covered in ice? Geologists Paul Hoffman and Dan Schrag suggest Earth was frozen solid until about 600 million years ago. They think Earth's climate changed by just a few degrees, but it was enough to make the ice caps cover the planet. The only life that survived was bacteria that were kept warm by volcanoes. And it was the volcanoes that changed the climate again, say Hoffman and Schrag. Suddenly eruptions melted the ice. Ocean levels rose. The scientists think this change might have taken only a hundred years. Not everyone agrees with the snowball hypothesis, but it could explain why new forms of life began to appear.

What Hit Them?

Not all scientists agree about what caused the Permian extinction. If an asteroid hit Earth, it would push massive amounts of dirt and dust into the air. This could block sunlight and create a cooler climate. An increase in volcanic eruptions is another possible cause.

The most famous extinction of all took place at the end of the Cretaceous Period. The extended winter that may have followed a meteor impact caused many large land animals—including dinosaurs—to become extinct.

In a new climate some species thrive and survive. They spread out and, over time, evolve to fill empty niches or unique roles in the environment. For example, before the Cretaceous extinction, the only mammals were small. After the dinosaurs became extinct, large mammals could fill the roles of large plant-eaters and meat-eaters.

Even today, climate change continues. Earth's average temperature rose about half a degree Celsius in the twentieth century. Studying how past climate changes shaped life helps scientists predict how it may affect us in the future.

A large plant-eating mammal, *Chalicotherium grande*, roamed Asia millions of years ago.

? UNANSWERED Questions

Scientists have learned a lot about climate change and mass extinctions by studying fossils. There are many questions still to be answered.

- What caused changes in Earth's climate?
- What else might have caused mass extinctions?
- How might climate change affect life on Earth in the future?

UNIT PROJECTS

As you study this unit, work alone or with a group on one of the projects listed below. Use the bulleted steps to guide your project.

Museum Display

What organisms survived the Permian extinction? What organisms went extinct?

- Create a museum display using art and text.
- Use visuals to show the organisms and the modern relatives that have close connections to them.

Design a Robot

Often, scientists design robots to study dangerous or distant locations.

- Design an artificial robot that would be well-adapted to survive an event that causes a mass extinction.
- Explain why the design would help the robot remain in operation.

Species over Time

Find out more about species that have gone extinct during recorded history.

- Choose one species that is now extinct.
- Present a timeline giving a history of that species.
- Describe what some of its ancestors and surviving related organisms are.
- Describe when it was last seen. Include some of the possible reasons for why it died out.

CAREER CENTER
CLASSZONE.COM

Learn more about careers in paleontology.

CHAPTER 1

The History of Life on Earth

the BIG idea

Living things, like Earth itself, change over time.

> How do scientists learn about the history of life on Earth?

Key Concepts

SECTION

1.1 **Earth has been home to living things for about 3.8 billion years.**
Learn how fossils help explain the development of life on Earth.

SECTION

1.2 **Species change over time.**
Learn how species develop and change.

SECTION

1.3 **Many types of evidence support evolution.**
Learn about the evidence scientists use to support evolution.

Internet Preview

CLASSZONE.COM

Chapter 1 online resources: Content Review, Simulation, Visualization, three Resource Centers, Math Tutorial, Test Practice

EXPLORE (the BIG idea)

What Can Rocks Show About Earth's History?

Look closely at two rocks from different places or at the two rocks below. What are the characteristics of each rock? Can you see evidence of living things in one of them?

Observe and Think
How could the evidence you gathered from your observations help you describe Earth's history?

Which One of These Things Is Not Like the Others?

Observe a handful of beans. Measure the length of each bean, observe the color, and note how many seeds are in each bean.

Observe and Think
What variety do you observe in the beans?

Investigate Activity: Matching Finch Beaks

Go to **Classzone.com** to match different finch beaks with the foods they eat. Learn how each type of beak functions.

Observe and Think
Can you think of any other beak types birds may have and how they relate to the food they eat?

NSTA
scilinks.org
SCi LINKS

The Fossil Record **Code: MDL036**

Getting Ready to Learn

◀ CONCEPT REVIEW

- Earth was formed over 4 billion years ago.
- Living things interact with their environment.

◀ VOCABULARY REVIEW

See Glossary for definitions.

cell	organism
DNA	species
genetic material	theory

CONTENT REVIEW
CLASSZONE.COM
Review concepts and vocabulary.

▶ TAKING NOTES

MAIN IDEA AND DETAILS

Make a two-column chart. Write the main ideas, such as those in the blue headings, in the column on the left. Write details about each of those main ideas in the column on the right.

VOCABULARY STRATEGY

Write each new vocabulary term in the center of a **frame game** diagram. Decide what information to frame it with. Use examples, descriptions, and parts of sentences that use the term in context or pictures. You can change the frame to fit each item.

See the Note-Taking Handbook on pages R45–R51.

SCIENCE NOTEBOOK

MAIN IDEAS	DETAILS
1. Fossils provide evidence of earlier life	1. Bones, prints, minerals
	1. Relative dating compares fossils
	1. Absolute dating uses the level of radioactivity

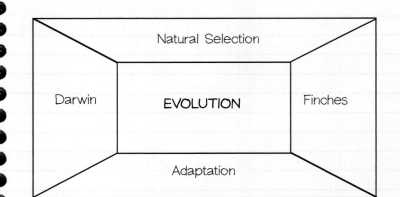

KEY CONCEPT

Earth has been home to living things for about 3.8 billion years.

◀ **BEFORE, you learned**

- Living things are diverse
- Living things share common characteristics
- A species is a group of living things that can breed with one another

▶ **NOW, you will learn**

- How scientists use fossils to learn about the history of life
- About patterns in the fossil record
- About mass extinctions

VOCABULARY

fossil p. 9
unicellular organism p. 12
multicellular
  organism p. 13
mass extinction p. 14

EXPLORE Fossils

What can you infer from the marks an object leaves behind?

PROCEDURE

1. Press a layer of clay into the petri dish.

2. Choose a small object and press it into the clay to make an imprint of your object.

3. Remove the object carefully and trade your imprint with a classmate.

WHAT DO YOU THINK?
- What object made the imprint?
- What do your observations indicate to you about how the imprint was formed?

MATERIALS
- clay
- petri dish
- small object

Fossils provide evidence of earlier life.

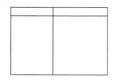

MAIN IDEA AND DETAILS
As you read this section, continue filling in the chart begun on page 8

Imagine watching a movie about the history of life on Earth. The beginning of the movie is set 3.8 billion years ago. At that time, the ocean would have been the setting. All living things lived in the sea. The end of the movie would show Earth today—a planet that is home to millions of species living on land as well as in water and air.

Of course, learning about the history of life isn't as easy as watching a movie. Modern ideas about life's history involve careful observation of the available evidence. Much of this evidence is provided by fossils. **Fossils** are the remains of organisms preserved in the earth. Fossils provide a glimpse of a very long story. In some ways, observing a fossil is like hitting the pause button on your video machine or looking at a snapshot of another time.

Bones, such as this jawbone, are a common type of fossil.

This fossil trilobite formed as minerals replaced the remains of the organism.

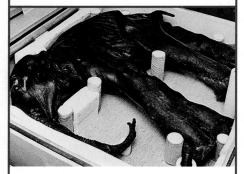

The preserved remains of ancient mammals, like the woolly mammoth, are rare.

VISUALIZATION
CLASSZONE.COM

Explore how a fossil can form.

Types of Fossils

You may have learned that fossils are the imprints or remains of once-living things. Most fossils are hard body parts such as bone. Perhaps you have seen displays of dinosaur skeletons in museums. These displays include fossil bones, such as the jawbone to the left. Other fossils form when minerals replace the remains of organisms or parts of organisms. The trilobite fossil shown in the middle photograph is an example of this type of fossil. Fossils also include prints made by organisms.

Very rarely, people find fossils that are the original remains of entire organisms. Explorers have found the frozen bodies of animals called woolly mammoths that lived about 10,000 years ago. The bodies of insects can be preserved in sap from plants.

Finding the Age of Fossils

How can scientists tell that the first organisms lived in oceans, or that dinosaurs lived on land and that they disappeared 65 million years ago? These questions and others can be addressed by determining the age of fossils. There are two approaches to dating fossils—relative dating and absolute dating. In relative dating, one fossil is compared with another fossil. The relative age tells you whether a fossil formed before or after another fossil.

The places where fossils are discovered provide information about their relative ages. Much of Earth's crust is rock, and rock forms over long periods of time. Understanding when and how rock forms gives scientists information about the sequence of events in Earth's history.

Materials such as sand and mud may settle to the bottom of a body of water. Over many millions of years, layers harden into rock. Shells and other remains of organisms can be trapped in those layers, forming fossils. Newer fossils are usually found in the top layers of rock, while older fossils are in the lower layers.

The absolute age of a fossil tells you when it was formed. To find the absolute age, scientists study the radioactive elements found in rocks and fossils. Some of these elements, such as uranium, decay at a very precise rate into more stable elements, such as lead. Thus, by measuring the amount of uranium and the amount of lead in an object, scientists can determine the object's age. The more lead it has, the older it is.

CHECK YOUR READING   What are the two ways scientists can determine the age of fossils?

INVESTIGATE Fossil Records

How do scientists interpret fossil evidence?

PROCEDURE

1. Individually examine each of your group's puzzle pieces. Consider the shape and size of each piece.

2. Arrange the pieces so that they fit together in the best possible way.

3. On the basis of your pieces, try to interpret what the overall puzzle picture may be.

4. Combine your puzzle pieces with another group's. Repeat steps 2 and 3.

WHAT DO YOU THINK?

- How did your interpretation of the puzzle picture change once you had more pieces to work with?

- Explain whether the gaps in the puzzle picture influenced your interpretation.

- Was it easier or more difficult to study the record with more "scientists" in your group?

CHALLENGE Brainstorm other ways scientists could learn about early life on Earth.

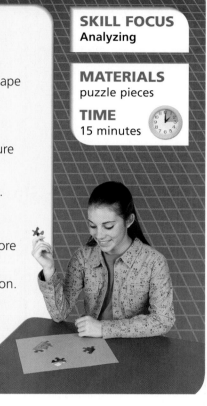

Assembling the Fossil Record

By combining absolute dating with relative dating, scientists can estimate the age of most fossils. The information about the fossils found in a particular location is called the fossil record. By assembling a fossil record, scientists can identify the periods of time during which different species lived and died. Scientists have used the fossil record to develop an overview of Earth's history.

READING TiP

A species is a group of organisms with similar characteristics that can interbreed.

Information from fossils helps scientists and artists describe wooly mammoths.

More complex organisms developed over time.

One of the most striking patterns that scientists find when they study the fossil record involves the development of more complex organisms. Below you will see how scientists have reconstructed the history of a modern city to show how life has developed over time. Recall that the first organisms were made up of single cells. Most organisms living today are single-celled. However, more and more species have developed more and more complex cells and structures over time.

Unicellular Organisms

READING TiP

Uni- means "single" and *multi-* means "several" or "many."

Unicellular organisms are organisms made up of a single cell. The organisms in the ocean 3.8 billion years ago were made of simple, single cells. Some of these organisms are responsible for the oxygen that now makes up our atmosphere. The early atmosphere did not contain as much oxygen as it now does. As the atmosphere changed, so did life on Earth.

Different types of single cells developed over time. Over millions of years the cells of organisms became more complex. Today, there are different species of life that include organisms made up of many cells.

Reconstructing the Past

Digging deep into the city of Denver, scientists have been able to reconstruct the ancient past.

55 million years ago The seas have been replaced by a tropical rain forest. The Rocky Mountains have been part of the landscape for over 10 million years.

70 million years ago Colorado is still flat and is now under a shallow sea. Sharks and marine lizards inhabit the water, and large reptiles fly overhead.

250 million years ago The area has no mountains and is covered in shallow, salty water. Unicellular organisms grow abundantly in the water.

Multicellular Organisms

Around 1.2 billion years ago, organisms made up of many cells began to live in Earth's oceans. **Multicellular organisms** are living things made up of many cells. Individual cells within multicellular organisms often perform specific tasks. For example, some cells may capture energy. Other cells might store materials. Still others might carry materials from one part of the organism to another. The most complex species of multicellular organisms have cells that are organized into tissues, organs, and systems.

Recall that all organisms have similar needs for energy, water, materials, and living space. For almost 3 billion years, these needs were met only in oceans. According to fossil records, the earliest multicellular organisms were tiny seaweeds. The earliest animals were similar to today's jellyfish.

Scientists learn about early life by studying different layers of rock

⬤ **CHECK YOUR READING** Explain how unicellular and multicellular organisms differ.

Life on Land

Consider the importance of water. Without it, you and most other living things would not be able to live. About 500 million years ago, the first multicellular organisms moved from water to land.

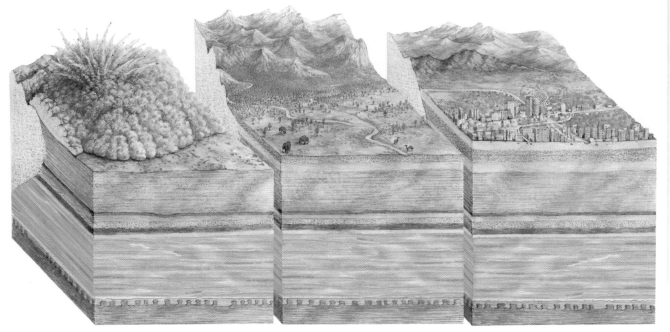

37 million years ago A volcanic eruption covers Colorado in a layer of hot ash, smothering plant and animal life.

16,000 years ago The plains look similar to what we see today—except that camels and mammoths roam the area.

Present day Buildings and highways cover the land. Humans have the technology to dig through layers of rock and reconstruct the past.

VOCABULARY
Remember to make a frame
game for the term *mass
extinction.*

In order to survive, these living things needed structures to help them get water. The first land-dwelling organisms were simple plants and fungi. Plants were able to obtain water from the soil through structures called roots. Fungi absorbed water from plants as well as from the soil. Insects were also probably among the first living things to inhabit land. Plants provided insects with food and shelter. After insects, animals such as amphibians and reptiles began living on land. They were followed by birds and mammals.

Earth's history includes mass extinctions.

About 10,000 years ago, the last woolly mammoth died without any offspring. At that time, the species became extinct, which means it disappeared. The only way that we know that some species, such as woolly mammoths, ever existed is through the fossil record. During Earth's history, there have been several periods when huge numbers of species have died or become extinct in a very short time. These events are called **mass extinctions.**

Although the fossil record shows a pattern of mass extinctions, two of these extinctions are particularly interesting. These are the Permian Extinction and the Cretaceous Extinction. The causes of these mass extinctions are not fully known.

Permian Extinction

About 250 million years ago, approximately 90 percent of the species living in the ocean became extinct. At the same time, many land-dwelling animals disappeared. Scientists who have studied Earth's history think that Earth's landmasses joined together, forming one enormous continent. This event would have changed the climate on land and the conditions within Earth's waters.

Cretaceous Extinction

Fossils show that around 140 million years ago, animals called dinosaurs lived all over the planet. However, the fossil record for dinosaurs ends about 65 million years ago. At the same time, more than half of the other species living on Earth became extinct.

How do scientists explain the extinction of so many species? One possibility is that a very large meteorite from space collided with Earth. The collision and its aftereffects wiped out most of the existing species. The remains of such a collision, the Chicxulub crater, can be found off the coast of Mexico. The computer graphic on page 15 shows the area of impact.

The largest mass extinction, the Permian Extinction, affected many different living things but it was the most devastating to organisms that lived in oceans.

Chicxulub Crater

Scientists think the impact of a meteorite off the coast of Mexico caused the Cretaceous extinction.

110 mi

The meteorite left a 200 km-wide crater off the Yucatán peninsula in Mexico.

Fragments from the meteorite have been found in the area.

The pattern in the fossil record shows that mass extinctions were followed by periods during which increasing numbers of new species developed. There may be a connection between the extinction of one species and the development of new species. For example, the extinction of dinosaurs may have made it possible for new species of mammals to develop.

CHECK YOUR READING What do scientists think caused the most recent mass extinction?

1.1 Review

KEY CONCEPTS

1. How do fossils help scientists understand the history of life?
2. How do scientists know that the first organisms were simple, unicellular organisms?
3. What is extinction? Give an example of a mass extinction and its results.

CRITICAL THINKING

4. **Synthesize** How do absolute dating and relative dating help scientists assemble a fossil record for an area?
5. **Sequence** Draw a timeline showing the sequence of three major events in the history of life. Include the following terms on your timeline: *unicellular, multicellular, ocean, land.*

CHALLENGE

6. **Predict** Using the Denver reconstruction as your model, explain how you would reconstruct the history of the environment in your town.

MATH TUTORIAL
CLASSZONE.COM
Click on Math Tutorial for more help writing and solving proportions.

This fossil is very similar to the modern snail shown above.

A Span of Time

The history of planet Earth spans from the present to about 5 billion years back. By comparison, the history of life on the planet spans about 4/5 of that time. Such a comparison is called a proportion.

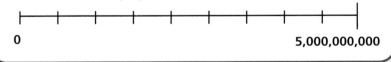

Example

To compare time spans in the history of Earth, you could make a meter-long timeline. Follow these steps:

(1) Measure and cut a piece of paper longer than 1 meter. Draw a straight line that is 1 meter long on your paper.

(2) Mark "0" at the far left to show the present day. Mark "5,000,000,000" at the right to show 5 billion years.

(3) Mark each centimeter along the line with a short stroke.

(4) Make a longer stroke at every 10 pencil marks. Your 5-billion-year span is now divided into 500-million-year sections. Each section is 1/10 in proportion to the total.

```
0                                        5,000,000,000
```

Label the timeline by answering the questions below.

1. Each short pencil stroke, or tick, represents 1/100 of the total span. How many years will each centimeter represent?

2. Each of the 10 long pencil marks should have its own label for the amount of time before the present day. The label for the first long pencil mark should be "500 million years." What numbers should label the others?

3. What fractions of the total span do the numbers in Question 2 represent?

CHALLENGE Copy and complete the table.

Event	Years Before Present Time	Number of cm from 0	Fraction of Total Time Span
Life appears on Earth.	3,800,000,000		
Multicellular life appears.	1,500,000,000		
First animals appear on land.	420,000,000		

Species change over time.

1.2

◀ **BEFORE,** you learned

- Fossils are evidence of earlier life
- More complex organisms have developed over time
- Mass extinctions contributed to the development of Earth's history

▶ **NOW,** you will learn

- About early ideas and observations on evolution
- How Darwin developed his theory of natural selection
- How new species arise from older species

VOCABULARY

evolution p. 17
natural selection p. 21
adaptation p. 22
speciation p. 24

THINK ABOUT

How have telephones changed over time?

Today people across the world can communicate in many different ways. One of the most common ways is over the telephone. Looking at the two pictures, can you describe how this form of communication has changed over time?

Scientists explore the concept of evolution.

MAIN IDEA AND DETAILS
Make a chart for the main idea *scientists explore the concept of evolution.* Include details about scientists' observations.

In a general sense, evolution involves a change over time. You could say that the way humans communicate has evolved. Certainly telephones have changed over time. The first telephones were the size of a shoebox. Today a telephone can fit in the palm of your hand and can send images as well as sound.

In biology, **evolution** refers to the process though which species change over time. The change results from a change in the genetic material of an organism and is passed from one generation to the next.

 What is evolution?

Early Ideas

READING TiP

The word *acquire* comes from the root meaning "to add to." Acquired traits are those that are "added" after an organism is born.

In the early 1800s, a French scientist named Jean Baptiste de Lamarck was the first scientist to propose a model of how life evolves. He became convinced that the fossil record showed that species had changed over time. He proposed an explanation for evolution based on the idea that an individual organism can acquire a new trait during its lifetime and then pass that trait on to its offspring. For example, Lamarck suggested that when giraffes stretched their necks to reach the leaves of tall trees, they passed the result of this stretching—a longer neck—to the next generation. Lamarck was a highly respected scientist, but he was unable to provide any evidence to support his idea.

CHECK YOUR READING How did Lamarck explain the process of evolution?

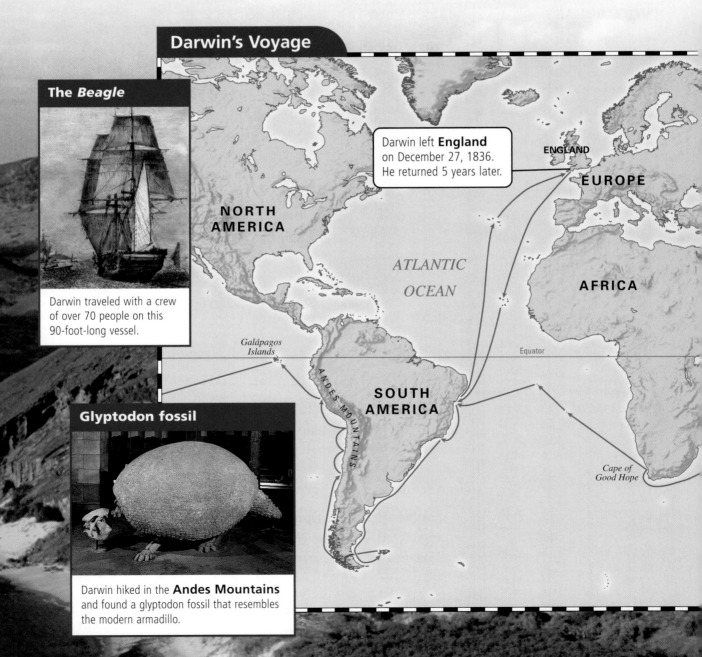

Darwin's Voyage

The *Beagle*

Darwin traveled with a crew of over 70 people on this 90-foot-long vessel.

Glyptodon fossil

Darwin hiked in the **Andes Mountains** and found a glyptodon fossil that resembles the modern armadillo.

Darwin left **England** on December 27, 1836. He returned 5 years later.

ENGLAND

EUROPE

NORTH AMERICA

ATLANTIC OCEAN

AFRICA

Galápagos Islands

Equator

ANDES MOUNTAINS

SOUTH AMERICA

Cape of Good Hope

Darwin's Observations

About 50 years after Lamarck, the British naturalist Charles Darwin published what would become the basis of the modern theory of evolution. As a young adult, Darwin spent 5 years as a naturalist aboard the *Beagle,* a ship in the British navy. The map below shows the route Darwin traveled. As he sailed along the coast of South America, he studied rock formations and collected fossils. He also began to compare the new animals he was seeing with ones from his own country.

The differences he saw in animals became more obvious when he visited the Galápagos Islands, a chain of volcanic islands about 950 kilometers (600 mi) off the South American coast. On the 18 Galápagos Islands, plants and animals not only differed from those he saw on the mainland, but some differed from island to island.

Darwin was only 20 in 1831 when he joined H.M.S. *Beagle.*

Distribution of Species

Platypus

Emu

At the end of his travels Darwin saw many plants and animals that were specific to certain continents, such as **Australia**. He was later able to explain this pattern with his theory of natural selection.

ASIA

INDIAN

OCEAN

Equator

PACIFIC OCEAN

AUSTRALIA

NEW ZEALAND

| 0 | 500 | 1000 miles |

| 0 | 500 | 1000 kilometers |

Darwin observed several types of tortoises on the islands. Tortoises with short necks were living in damp areas with abundant plant life that grew close to the ground. Longer-necked tortoises were living in dry areas with cacti. He considered whether the length of their necks made it possible for the tortoises to live in different environments.

Darwin also found many different types of birds called finches living on the islands. Some finches were common in the treetops, while others lived in the lower shrubs of a neighboring island. Among the different islands he noticed a variety of beak shapes and sizes. Some finches had heavy, short beaks useful for pecking trees or seeds, while others had small, thin beaks that could be used for capturing insects. These observations caused Darwin to wonder if the birds had evolved from similar species.

Darwin's Finches

On the Galápagos Islands, Darwin observed similar-looking birds with very different beaks. These birds are closely related finch species that are suited to different habitats on the island.

Woodpecker Finch

Vegetarian Finch

The woodpecker finch is able to hold a twig in its long pointed beak, which it uses to pull the larvas of insects from a tree. The vegetarian finch has a curved beak, ideal for taking large berries from a branch.

Large Ground Finch

Cactus Finch

The large ground finch has a large beak that it uses to crack open the hard shells of the seeds it feeds on. The cactus finch has a narrow beak that it uses to cut into a cactus and eat the tissue inside.

Natural selection explains how living things evolve.

After Darwin returned home to England in 1836, he spent several years analyzing the observations and specimens he had collected on his voyage. He struggled to develop an explanation that would account for the amazing diversity of species he saw and for the relationships between them. By 1844 he had developed a hypothesis based in part on an insight from one of his hobbies—breeding pigeons.

Darwin knew from personal experience that breeders can produce new varieties of an animal over time. The process breeders use is called artificial selection. For example, breeders produce a new breed of dog by selecting dogs that have certain desired traits and then allowing only those individuals to mate. From the resulting litters, they again selectively breed only the individual dogs with the desired traits. By repeating this process generation after generation, a new breed is produced.

RESOURCE CENTER
CLASSZONE.COM
Learn more about natural selection.

 CHECK YOUR READING What is artificial selection?

Artificial Selection

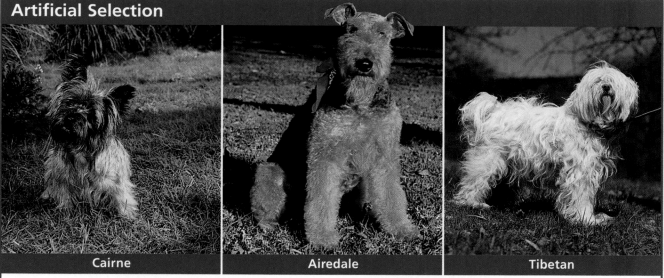

Cairne Airedale Tibetan

COMPARE AND CONTRAST These dogs are all terriers, but they have been bred through artificial selection to show very specific traits. How are the dogs similar? How are they different?

Darwin's insight was that a similar process might be going on in nature. He proposed that, through a process he called **natural selection,** members of a species that are best suited to their environment survive and reproduce at a higher rate than other members of the species. Darwin based this idea on a few key principles. These are overproduction, variation, adaptation, and selection.

Overproduction

Take a look at how Darwin's ideas are useful for the study of salmon. When a plant or an animal reproduces, it usually makes more offspring than the environment can support, as you can see in the diagram on page 23. A female salmon may lay several thousand fertile eggs, but not all of them will hatch. Only a few hundred of the salmon that hatch from the eggs will survive disease and avoid fish-eating predators. Several dozen of these survivors will live to adulthood. An even smaller number will successfully reproduce.

Variation

READING TiP

As you read about the principles of natural selection, refer to the diagrams on page 23.

Within a species there are natural differences, or variations, in traits. For example, if you looked very closely at thousands of salmon, you might see slight differences among individuals. Some might have larger fins. Others might have distinct patterns of spots on their scales. Many of the differences among individuals result from differences in the genetic material of the fish.

Sometimes the genetic material itself changes, causing a new variation to come about. A change in the genetic material is referred to as a mutation. As the fish with the new variation reproduces, the trait gets passed on to its offspring. Therefore, genetic variations are passed on from one generation to the next.

Adaptation

Sometimes a mutation occurs that makes an individual better able to survive than other members of the group. An **adaptation** is any inherited trait that gives an organism an advantage in its particular environment. For example, a slight change in the shape of a tail fin may increase a fish's chance of survival by helping it swim faster and avoid predators.

Selection

Darwin reasoned that individual organisms with a particular adaptation are most likely to survive long enough to reproduce. As a result, the adaptation becomes more common in the next generation of offspring. As this process repeats from generation to generation, more members of a species show the adaptation. Consider the shape of the salmon. If a change in the tail fin makes the salmon better able to move upstream and lay eggs, scientists say this trait has been selected for in this environment. In other words, the species is evolving through natural selection.

Natural Selection

Certain traits become more common in a group of organisms through the process of natural selection.

Overproduction

A fish may lay hundreds of eggs, but only a small number will survive to reach adulthood.

Variation

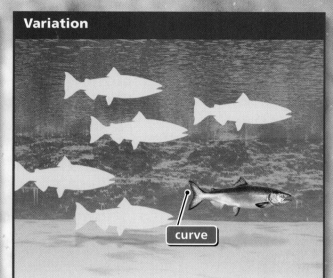

A mutation may cause a slight curve to develop in a fish's tail.

Adaptation

The fish with the curved tail is able to swim more quickly and so escapes predators. The fish reproduces.

Selection

With each generation, more fish with a curved tail survive to reproduce. Over time, they make up a larger part of the group.

READING VISUALS How does natural selection occur for an individual salmon?

New species develop from earlier species.

Darwin's personal observations and the work of another scientist, Alfred Wallace, led Darwin to write about this new concept of evolution. In 1859, after more than twenty years of work, Darwin published his ideas in his book *On the Origin of Species.* This work led the way for our modern understanding of how new species arise.

Speciation

Speciation is the evolution of new species from an existing species. Speciation may occur when the environment changes dramatically, or when the environment changes gradually. The Galápagos finch populations Darwin studied showed evidence of speciation.

Isolation

Darwin's trip to the Galápagos Islands showed him an important point about speciation. Many new species had evolved after populations were separated from the mainland and were not able to breed with their mainland relatives. Darwin reasoned that isolation of populations by geographical or other barriers could contribute to the process of speciation. A species of fish called cichlids shows how a physical barrier contributes to speciation.

Speciation

In this African lake, new species of cichlids have evolved.

LAKE TANGANYIKA

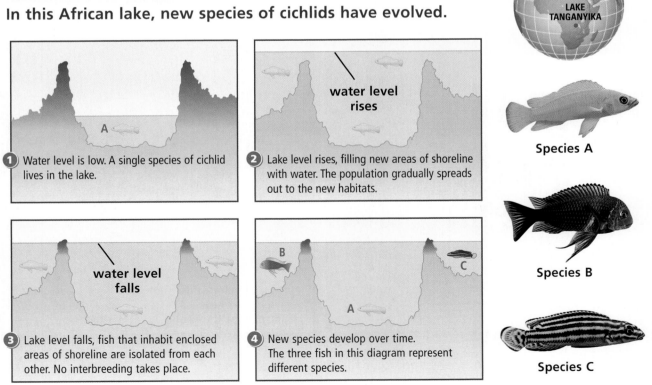

1. Water level is low. A single species of cichlid lives in the lake.

2. Lake level rises, filling new areas of shoreline with water. The population gradually spreads out to the new habitats.

water level rises

3. Lake level falls, fish that inhabit enclosed areas of shoreline are isolated from each other. No interbreeding takes place.

water level falls

4. New species develop over time. The three fish in this diagram represent different species.

Species A

Species B

Species C

In Lake Tanganyika, one of the largest lakes in the world, there are over 150 species of cichlids. Members of one particular genus, *tropheus*, originally lived along the rocky shore and couldn't cross the open water. The climate and geology of the area caused the lake's water level to rise and fall many times over thousands of years. As the water level changed, a new, rocky habitat was formed, and some populations of cichlids became isolated from each other.

The isolated populations were unable to interact with each other because they couldn't cross open waters. As a result, genetic differences began to add up in these populations. The cichlid populations now represent distinct species. They have developed unique characteristics and cannot breed with each other. See diagram on page 24.

Today scientists understand that isolation is essential to speciation. For a species to separate, two populations must be prevented from reproducing with each other. A geographic boundary like an ocean or mountain range can result in isolation. Two populations of a species can also be isolated if they feed on different things or reproduce at different times of the year.

The Rocky Mountains are an example of a barrier that can isolate populations.

As the cichlids in Lake Tanganyika show, the mutations in one isolated group may differ from another. Two or more populations may evolve differently from each other. The result is speciation, which has contributed to the biodiversity on Earth.

 CHECK YOUR READING What is a key factor that can lead to speciation?

1.2 Review

KEY CONCEPTS

1. How did Lamarck's ideas differ from Darwin's?

2. What did Darwin observe in the finch populations that supported his idea of natural selection?

3. Explain how isolation helps speciation.

CRITICAL THINKING

4. **Hypothesize** Two species of grasses are separated by a tall mountain range. A third species of grass shares some characteristics with each of the other two species. It inhabits a small valley, surrounded on all sides by mountains. Form a hypothesis for the origin of the third species.

⬤ CHALLENGE

5. **Predict** The Arctic hare lives in snow-covered mountains in Canada. The hare is hunted by foxes, wolves, and owls. Which trait is more likely to be inherited by new generations of hares: white fur or black fur?

CHAPTER INVESTIGATION

Modeling Natural Selection

OVERVIEW AND PURPOSE Organisms that are best adapted to their environment tend to survive and reproduce. In this lab you will

- play a game that models the effect of natural selection in an environment
- determine what happens to a group of organisms as a result of natural selection

▶ Question

Write It Up

As you read the steps to the game, think about what makes a population successful in an environment. How will the game model natural selection?

MATERIALS
- pair of number cubes
- 16 red paper clips
- 16 blue paper clips
- 16 yellow paper clips

▶ Procedure

1. Make a game board like the one shown below. In your **Science Notebook** make a table like the one on page 27 to record your data.

	1	2	3	4
1				
2				
3				
4				

2. Count out 10 red paper clips, 4 blue paper clips, and 2 yellow paper clips. Randomly place the paper clips on the board. Keep the rest of the paper clips in a reserve pile.

3 Each color represents a different population of a single species. The board represents the environment. Roll the number cubes to determine which paper clips "live," or remain on the board, and which paper clips "die," or are removed from the board. Predict which color paper clip you think will be the last remaining color. Write down your prediction.

4 Roll the number cubes to determine which square, or part of the environment, will be affected. For example, 2,3 indicates the paper clip in column 2, row 3. If the numbers 5 or 6 come up, roll again until you have a number between 1 and 4 for each cube.

5 Now roll one cube to see what will happen to the paper clip or organism in that square. Use the chart below to determine if the paper clip "lives" or "dies." If the paper clip lives, repeat steps 4 and 5 until one paper clip dies, or is removed from the board. In your table, record which colors live and die.

Red	Remove if you roll a 1, 2, 3, 4, or 5.
Blue	Remove if you roll a 1, 2, or 3.
Yellow	Remove if you roll a 1 or 2.

6 Now that a paper clip has been removed, you need to see what population will reproduce to fill that space. Roll both cubes to choose another square. The color of the paper clip in that square represents the population that will "reproduce." Pick the same color paper clip from your reserve pile and place it on the empty square. All squares on the board should always have a paper clip.

7 Continue playing the game by repeating steps 4–6 until all the paper clips on the board are the same color.

▶ Observe and Analyze

1. **OBSERVE** Which color paper clip filled the board at the end of the game?

2. **PREDICT** Compare the results with your prediction. Do the results support your prediction?

▶ Conclude

1. **INFER** What does the random selection by rolling both number cubes represent? Explain.

2. **INFER** If the individual paper clips represent different members of a single species, then what might the different colors represent?

3. **LIMITATIONS** What problems or sources of error exist in this model? Give examples.

4. **APPLY** How does this game model natural selection?

▶ INVESTIGATE Further

CHALLENGE Occasionally mutations occur in a population that can either help or damage the population's chance of survival. Add another step to the game that would account for mutations.

Modeling Natural Selection

Table 1. Patterns in a Population

Paper Clip Color	Live	Die

1.3
Many types of evidence support evolution.

BEFORE, you learned

- Natural selection explains part of the process of evolution
- New species develop from earlier species

NOW, you will learn

- How scientists develop theories
- About the evidence Darwin used to support evolution
- About additional evidence most scientists use today

VOCABULARY

ancestor p. 29
vestigial organ p. 30
gene p. 33

EXPLORE Evidence

How can observations supply evidence?

PROCEDURE

① Consider the following statement: It rained last night.

② Look at the following observations and determine which pieces of evidence support the statement.
- There are puddles on the ground.
- The weather report says there will be scattered showers today.
- Your sister tells you there was a rain delay during last night's tennis match.

MATERIALS
- paper
- pencil

WHAT DO YOU THINK?

- What other observations can you come up with that would supply evidence for the first statement?
- Could any of the evidence be misleading?

Observations provide evidence for theories.

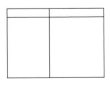

MAIN IDEA AND DETAILS
Don't forget to make a chart of details supporting the main idea that observations provide evidence for theories. Include a definition of *theory* in your chart.

In this chapter, you've learned about important observations that scientists have used to understand the history of living things. These observations provided Darwin with information he used to describe his ideas about evolution.

Darwin, like all good scientists, was skeptical about his observations and conclusions. Although the historic trip on the *Beagle* took place between 1831 and 1836, Darwin didn't publish the book explaining his theory until 1859. In order to understand the importance of Darwin's work, it is also important to understand the meaning of the term *theory*.

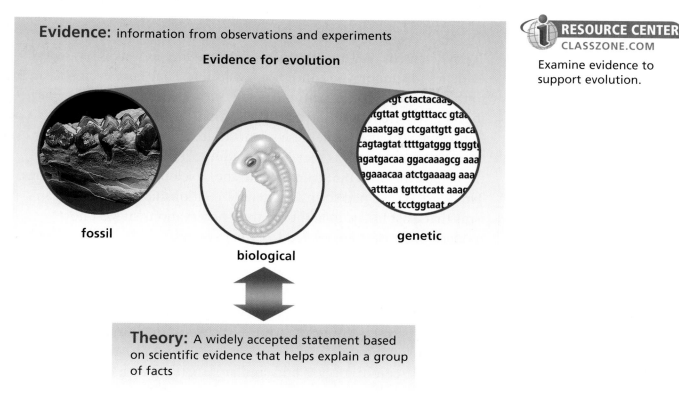

Evidence: information from observations and experiments

Evidence for evolution

fossil

biological

genetic

RESOURCE CENTER
CLASSZONE.COM

Examine evidence to support evolution.

Theory: A widely accepted statement based on scientific evidence that helps explain a group of facts

A scientific theory is a statement based on observation and experiment. If continued observation and experiment support the statement, it may become widely accepted. A theory that has been widely accepted is used to explain and predict natural phenomena. The chart above will help give you an idea of how a theory works and what evidence has been used to support evolution and the theory of natural selection.

CHECK YOUR READING How do scientists support theories?

Fossil evidence supports evolution.

You have read that Darwin collected many specimens of fossils on his trip. These specimens provided evidence that species existing in the past were very similar to species living during Darwin's time. For example, the fossil of an extinct animal called the glyptodon resembles the modern armadillo, an animal found today in South America.

The geographic information about many fossils provides evidence that two species with a common ancestor can develop differently in different locations. An **ancestor** is an early form of an organism from which later forms descend. The idea of common ancestors is important to the theory of natural selection and to the evidence that supports the theory. Scientists comparing modern plants and modern algae to fossil algae can tell that they all share a common ancestor.

CHECK YOUR READING What is a common ancestor?

Biological evidence supports evolution.

Today scientists continue to study fossil evidence as well as biological evidence to support the concept of evolution. They have even returned to the Galápagos to further investigate Darwin's work. What they have found gives strength to the theory he proposed nearly 150 years ago. Returning year after year, these scientists are able to follow and record evolutionary changes as they are unfolding. The biological evidence they study includes the structure and the development of living things. This work has helped scientists identify relationships between organisms that exist today. In addition, their observations suggest how modern organisms are related to earlier species.

Similarities in Structure

Evidence for evolution can be observed within the physical structures of adult organisms. Scientists who study evolution and development consider two types of structural evidence. They are vestigial (veh-STIHJ-ee-uhl) organs and similar structures with different functions.

 CHECK YOUR READING What are two types of structural evidence?

READING TiP

The root of the word vestigial means "footprint." A vestige refers to visible evidence that is left behind—such as a footprint.

Vestigial organs are physical structures that were fully developed and functional in an ancestral group of organisms but are reduced and unused in the later species. In the bodies of whales there are small leg bones that are vestigial. The skeletons of snakes also have traces of leglike structures that are not used. These vestigial organs help researchers see how some modern organisms are related to ancestors that had similar structures.

Similar structures with different functions Scientists studying the anatomy of living things have also noticed that many different species share similar structures. But these structures are used differently by each species. For example, lizards, bats, and manatees have forelimbs that have a similar bone structure. As you can see from the diagram on page 31, there is one short bone and one long bone that go from a shoulder structure to a wrist structure. But obviously, a lizard, a bat, and a manatee use this structure in different ways.

This similarity in structure indicates that these organisms shared a common ancestor. The process of natural selection caused the variations in form and function that can be observed today. These organisms lived in different environments and so were under different pressures. For lizards the environment was land, for bats it was the air, and for manatees the water. The environment influenced the selection of traits.

Biological Evidence for Evolution

Scientists learn about common ancestors by looking at physical structures.

Vestigial Structures

The small, leglike bones in modern whales indicate that an early ancestor may have had legs.

Ambulocetus, an extinct whalelike animal with four legs

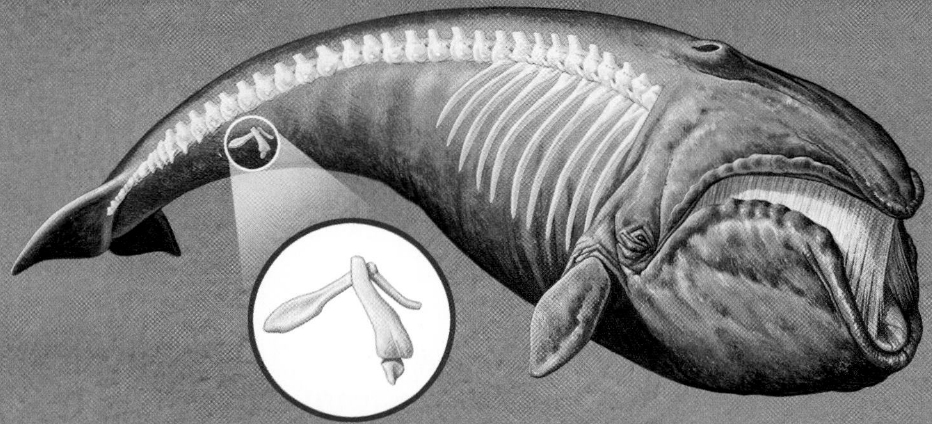

modern whale

Similar Structures, Different Functions

gecko lizard

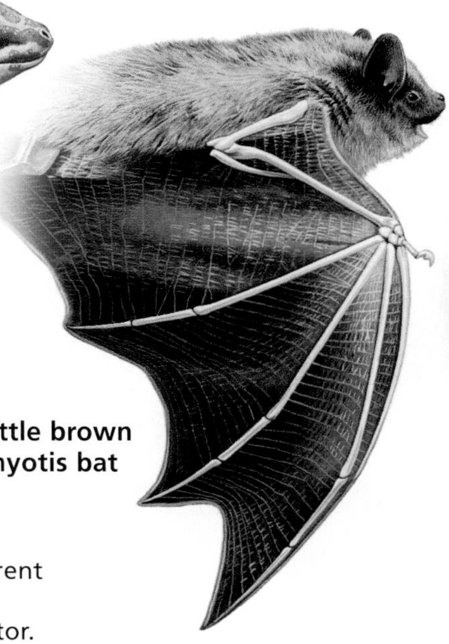

little brown myotis bat

manatee

These animals share a similar bone structure that they use in very different ways. The presence of this similar structure indicates a common ancestor.

Similarities in Development

READING TiP

As you read about the development of a chicken, rabbit, and salamander, study the diagram below.

Scientists in the 1700s were fascinated by the fact that various animals looked similar in their earliest stages of life. They noted that as the organisms developed, they became less and less alike. Today's scientists continue to compare the developmental stages of different species.

The adult stages of many species do not look similar. For example, a rabbit does not look anything like a chicken. However, study reveals that the early life stages of a chicken and a rabbit are similar. An organism that is in an early stage of development is called an embryo.

In the diagram below, notice the development of three different species: a chicken, a rabbit, and a salamander. In the early stages of development, the embryos of all three organisms look similar. As they continue to develop, they begin to take on distinct characteristics. The chicken has a structure that starts to resemble a beak. The salamander begins to look as if it is adapted for life near water. In their adult stages, these three species no longer look similar.

Similarities in Development

The study of embryos shows that animals that appear to be very different as adults are similar during early development.

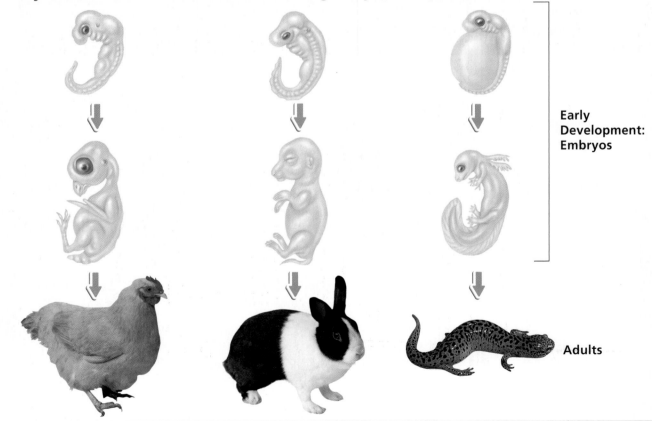

Early Development: Embryos

Adults

How can a sequence communicate information?

PROCEDURE

1. From your pile of letters (A, D, E, R), spell out the word RED.

2. Working with a partner, use the letters to spell two more words having three letters.

WHAT DO YOU THINK?

How does rearranging the letters change the meaning of the words?

CHALLENGE Cut out words from a newspaper. Arrange these words to form different phrases. How do these phrases communicate different messages?

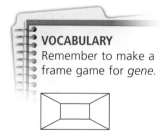

SKILL FOCUS
Sequencing

MATERIALS
letter cards

TIME
20 minutes

Genetic evidence supports evolution.

The key to understanding how traits are passed from one generation to the next lies in the study of DNA, the genetic material found in all organisms. DNA contains the information all organisms need to grow and to maintain themselves. When organisms reproduce, they pass on their genetic material to their offspring.

DNA contains a code that a cell uses to put together all the materials it needs to function properly. The code is made up of four different chemical subunits called bases. The bases are symbolized by the four letters A, T, C, and G. Located within DNA are individual genes. A **gene** is a segment of DNA that relates to a specific trait or function of an organism. Each gene has a particular sequence of bases. The cell takes this sequence and translates it into the chemicals and structures the organism needs.

Scientists studying genes have identified a gene called the clock gene in many mammals. This particular gene relates to the function of sleeping and waking. As scientists learn more they can identify patterns of behavior in different organisms. The chart on page 34 compares the DNA sequence of part of the clock gene in both humans and mice.

VOCABULARY
Remember to make a frame game for *gene*.

 CHECK YOUR READING   What is a gene?

Comparing Genes

Humans and mice look very different, but the DNA that makes up their genes is surprisingly similar.

DNA Sequence

clock gene sequence begins here

Human	gtacaaatgt	ctactacaag	acgaaaacgt	agtatgttat	gttgtttacc	gtaagctgta
Mouse	gtacaaatgt	ctaccacaag	acgaaaacat	aatgtgttat	ggtgtttacc	gtaagctgta
Human	gtaaaatgag	ctcgattgtt	gacagagatg	acagtagtat	ttttgatggg	ttggtggaag
Mouse	gtaaaatgag	ctcaattgtt	gacagagatg	acagtagtat	ttttgatgga	ttggtggaag
Human	aagatgacaa	ggacaaagcg	aaaagagtat	ctagaaacaa	atctgaaaag	aaacgtagag
Mouse	aagatgacaa	ggacaaagca	aaaagagtat	ctagaaacaa	atcagaaaag	aaacgtagag
Human	atcaatttaa	tgttctcatt	aaagaactgg	gatccatgct	tcctggtaat	gctagaaaga
Mouse	atcagttcaa	tgtcctcatt	aaggagctgg	ggtctatgct	tcctggtaac	gcgagaaaga

The bar shows where the mouse and human DNA are different.

The letters represent different subunits of DNA.

Scientists can tell how closely organisms are related by comparing their DNA. The more matches there are in the sequence of bases between two organisms, the more closely related they are. For example, almost all the genes found in a mouse are also found in a human. Even though the two organisms appear so different, much of the functioning of their cells is similar.

1.3 Review

KEY CONCEPTS

1. Describe in your own words how scientists use the word *theory*.

2. What type of evidence did Darwin use to support his theory of evolution?

3. Identify three different types of evidence that today's scientists use to support the theory of evolution.

CRITICAL THINKING

4. **Analyze** Describe three characteristics of a scientific theory. Explain how Darwin's theory of evolution is an example of a scientific theory.

⬤ CHALLENGE

5. **Predict** If you were looking at the sequence within the genes of two species, how would you predict that the two species are related?

How Did the Deep-Sea Angler Get Its Glow?

A fish that uses a fishing pole to catch food might seem odd. However, anglerfish do just that. The fish have a modified spine that extends from their head, almost like a fishing pole. At the end is a small piece of tissue that is similar in shape to a small worm. The tissue functions like a lure that a fisherman uses to catch fish. The anglerfish wiggles its "lure" to attract prey. If the prey fish moves in close enough, the anglerfish opens its mouth and swallows the prey whole. The "fishing poles" of abyssal anglerfish, anglerfish that live in the deep sea, have an interesting adaptation. The "lure" actually glows in the dark—it is bioluminescent.

▶ Observations

From laboratory research and field studies, scientists made these observations.

> There are more than 200 species of anglerfish. Many of these live in deep water.
>
> Shallow-water species do not have glow-in-the-dark "lures."
>
> Only female abyssal anglerfish have a "pole." They do not have pelvic fins and are not strong swimmers.
>
> Other deep-sea organisms, including bacteria, jellyfish, even some squid, are bioluminescent.

▶ Hypotheses

Consider these hypotheses.

> The ancestors of abyssal anglerfish lived in shallow waters. Some of these fish drifted into deep waters. A bioluminescent lure helped some survive.
>
> Light does not reach down to the bottom of the deep sea. Bioluminescence provides an advantage for the anglerfish because it makes its lure noticeable.
>
> A bioluminescent lure is more valuable to a female abyssal anglerfish than the ability to swim.

▶ Evaluate Each Hypothesis

On Your Own For each hypothesis, think about whether all the observations support it. Some facts may rule out some hypotheses. Others may support them.

As a Group Decide which hypothesis is the most reasonable. Discuss your thinking and conclusions in a small group and see if the group can agree.

Chapter Review

the **BIG** idea

Living things, like Earth itself, change over time.

CONTENT REVIEW
CLASSZONE.COM

KEY CONCEPTS SUMMARY

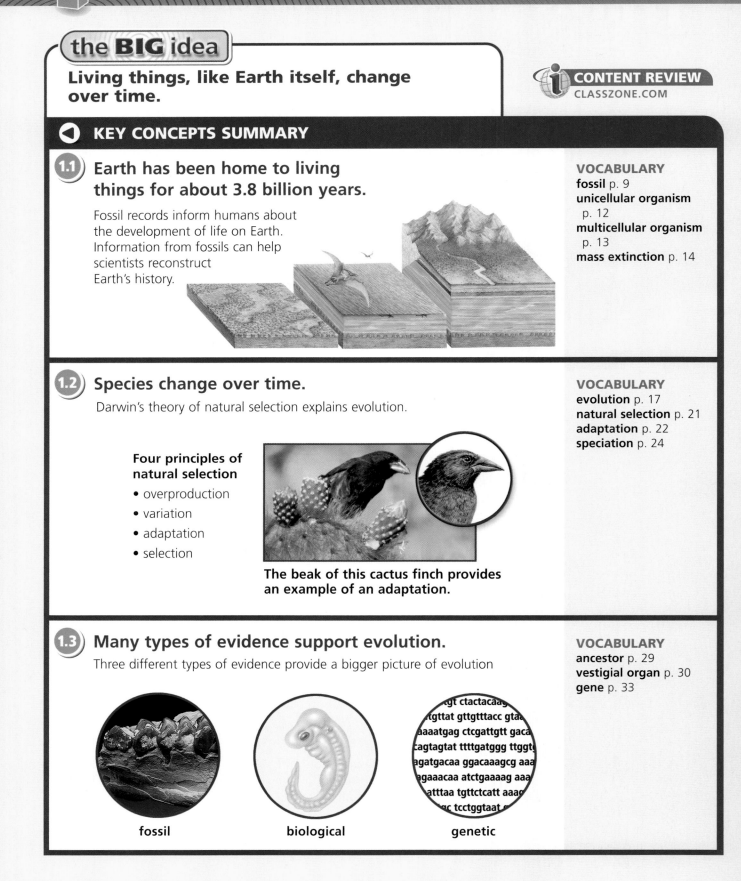

1.1 **Earth has been home to living things for about 3.8 billion years.**

Fossil records inform humans about the development of life on Earth. Information from fossils can help scientists reconstruct Earth's history.

VOCABULARY
fossil p. 9
unicellular organism p. 12
multicellular organism p. 13
mass extinction p. 14

1.2 **Species change over time.**

Darwin's theory of natural selection explains evolution.

Four principles of natural selection
- overproduction
- variation
- adaptation
- selection

The beak of this cactus finch provides an example of an adaptation.

VOCABULARY
evolution p. 17
natural selection p. 21
adaptation p. 22
speciation p. 24

1.3 **Many types of evidence support evolution.**

Three different types of evidence provide a bigger picture of evolution

fossil   biological   genetic

gt ctactacaag
tgttat gttgtttacc gta
aaaatgag ctcgattgtt gaca
cagtagtat ttttgatggg ttggt
agatgacaa ggacaaagcg aaa
agaaacaa atctgaaaag aaa
atttaa tgttctcatt aaaa
c tcctggtaat

VOCABULARY
ancestor p. 29
vestigial organ p. 30
gene p. 33

Reviewing Vocabulary

Draw a triangle for each of the terms below. On the wide bottom of the triangle, write the term and your own definition of it. Above that, write a sentence in which you use the term correctly. At the top of the triangle, draw a small picture to show what the term looks like.

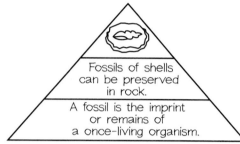

Fossils of shells can be preserved in rock.

A fossil is the imprint or remains of a once-living organism.

1. unicellular organism

2. multicellular organism

3. adaptation

4. vestigial structure

Reviewing Key Concepts

Multiple Choice *Choose the letter of the best answer.*

5. Which is *not* part of the fossil record?
   a. fossil bones
   b. preserved remains
   c. living unicellular organisms
   d. imprints

6. Whether a fossil formed before or after another fossil is described by its
   a. relative age
   b. absolute age
   c. fossil record
   d. radioactive age

7. The earliest multicellular organisms were
   a. jellyfish
   b. simple plants
   c. fungi
   d. tiny seaweeds

8. Which is a possible explanation for mass extinctions?
   a. Earth had no water.
   b. A meteorite collided with Earth.
   c. The continents separated.
   d. Woolly mammoths left no offspring.

9. Darwin's theory that species develop new traits and change over time is known as
   a. natural selection
   c. speciation
   b. evolution
   d. adaptation

10. Which describes Lamarck's explanation for changes in the fossil record?
    a. Species best suited to their environments survive better than others.
    b. Variation within a species can be passed on to offspring.
    c. Acquired traits are passed on from one generation to another.
    d. Giraffes adapted to their environment.

11. A slight change in a rabbit's ability to hear its predators better and help it survive is
    a. an adaptation
    b. a vestigial structure
    c. an aquired trait
    d. an isolation

12. Which is necessary for speciation to occur?
    a. adaptation
    b. mass extinction
    c. isolation
    d. acquired traits

13. Which of the following statements explain why the theory of evolution is widely accepted by the scientific community?
    a. It has been proven by experiments.
    b. The fossil record is complete.
    c. It is supported by genetic evidence.
    d. Lamarck's theory was correct.

14. Genetic evidence is based on the study of
    a. embryonic development
    b. mutations
    c. common ancestors
    d. DNA sequences

15. Genetic information that cells use to control the production of new cells is located in

   a. embryos

   b. genes

   c. the environment

   d. vestigial structures

Short Answer *Write a short answer to each question.*

16. Describe how the relative age of a fossil is determined by studying layers of rock.

17. Explain the difference between artificial selection and natural selection.

18. How does common ancestry between two species support evolution?

Thinking Critically

19. **COMMUNICATE** What have scientists learned about past life on Earth from the fossil record?

20. **PROVIDE EXAMPLES** Explain the principle of overproduction. Give an example.

21. **SYNTHESIZE** How might the mass extinction of dinosaurs enable many new species of mammals to develop?

22. **EVALUATE** How would natural selection have led to the development of giraffes with long necks as opposed to giraffes with short necks?

23. **PROVIDE EXAMPLES** How are variation and adaptations related to natural selection? Give an example.

24. **PREDICT** In Africa's Lake Tanganyika different populations of cichlids became isolated from each other. Based on what you already learned, predict how the changing water level helped the cichlid population to change. How do you think the development of new cichlid species affected other living things in the lake?

25. **ANALYZE** How is geographic isolation related to the formation of a new species?

26. **EVALUATE** Pandas were once considered to be closely related to raccoons and red pandas because of their physical similarities. Today, scientists have learned that pandas are more closely related to bears than to raccoons and red pandas. What evidence might scientists have used to draw this conclusion? Explain.

27. **INFER** What does the presence of similar structures in two—organisms such as a dolphin's flipper and a lizard's forelimb—indicate?

the BIG idea

28. **INFER** Look again at the picture on pages 6–7. Now that you have finished the chapter, how would you change or add details to your answer to the question on the photograph?

29. **SYNTHESIZE** The beaks of hummingbirds are adapted to fit into long, thin flowers. Hummingbirds can feed on the nectar inside the flower. Write an explanation for this adaptation that Lamarck might have proposed. Then write an explanation for this adaptation based on Darwin's ideas. Use the terms acquired traits and natural selection in your answer.

UNIT PROJECTS

If you are doing a unit project, make a folder for your project. Include in your folder a list of the resources you will need, the date on which the project is due, and a schedule to track your progress. Begin gathering data.

Interpreting Diagrams

Choose the letter of the best answer.

This diagram shows how groups of carnivores are related to one another. Each Y in the diagram indicates a common ancestor.

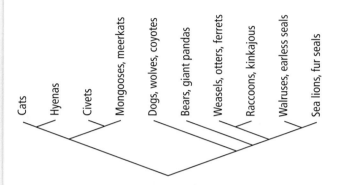

1. Hyenas are most closely related to which group?
   a. cats
   b. civets
   c. mongooses and meerkats
   d. raccoons and kinkajous

2. Weasels, otters, and ferrets are most closely related to
   a. bears and giant pandas
   b. sea lions and fur seals
   c. raccoons and kinkajous
   d. mongooses and meerkats

3. Sea lions and fur seals share their closest common ancestor with
   a. walruses and earless seals
   b. raccoons and kinkajous
   c. mongoose and muskrats
   d. civets

4. Which statement is true based on the information in the diagram?
   a. Dogs, wolves, and coyotes do not share a common ancestor with any of the groups.
   b. Raccoons are more closely related to weasels than they are to giant pandas.
   c. None of the groups shown in the diagram share a common ancestor.
   d. Mongooses and meerkats are the same as civets.

5. The branches on the diagram indicate where
   a. mass extinctions might have occurred
   b. speciation took place
   c. groups acquired traits and passed them onto their offspring
   d. there are gaps in the line of evolution

Extended Response

6. A scientist has discovered a new type of animal in the tundra area near the North Pole. Write a paragraph describing the type of evidence the scientist might use to classify the animal by its evolutionary history in the chart shown. Use these terms in your paragraph. Underline each term in your answer.

| embryo | DNA sequences |
| vestigial structures | common ancestor |

7. Write a paragraph in which you describe the traits of one of the animals named in the diagram. Choose several traits and describe how these traits might help the animal survive. Then describe how these might have been the result of adaptations and natural selection.

Classification of Living Things

the **BIG** idea

Scientists have developed a system for classifying the great diversity of living things.

Key Concepts

Internet Preview

CLASSZONE.COM

Chapter 2 online resources: Content Review, Simulation, 3 Resource Centers, Math Tutorial, Test Practice

How many different types of organisms do you see and how would you group them?

EXPLORE (the BIG idea)

How Are Fingerprints Different?

Make fingerprints of your thumb and the thumbs of several class-mates on separate index cards.

Observe and Think What traits do all finger-prints have in common? What traits of finger-prints allow you to tell them apart?

How Would You Sort Pennies?

Place 20 pennies in a plastic cup. Place your hand over the cup and shake it. Gently pour the pennies onto a table. Without flipping the pennies over, use one trait of the pennies to sort them into groups A and B. Again, without flipping them over, use a second trait to sort the pennies in group A into groups A1 and A2.

Observe and Think What traits do the pen-nies in each group share? Which group has the largest numbers of pennies?

Internet Activity: Linnaeus

Go to Classzone.com to learn more about Carolus Linnaeus, who, over 200 years ago, laid the groundwork for how today's scientists classify things.

Observe and Think What evidence did Linnaeus use to classify organisms?

NSTA
scilinks.org
SCiLINKS

Classification Systems **Code: MDL037**

Getting Ready to Learn

CONCEPT REVIEW

- Species change over time.
- Fossils and other evidence show that species change.
- New species develop from ancestral species.

VOCABULARY REVIEW

evolution p. 17

ancestor p. 29

See Glossary for definitions.

species, trait, DNA

CONTENT REVIEW
CLASSZONE.COM

Review concepts and vocabulary.

TAKING NOTES

SUPPORTING MAIN IDEAS

Make a chart to show main ideas and the information that supports them. Copy each blue heading. Below each heading, add supporting information, such as reasons, explanations, and examples.

VOCABULARY STRATEGY

Place each vocabulary term at the center of a **description wheel** diagram. Write some words describing it on the spokes.

See the Note-Taking Handbook on pages R45–R51.

SCIENCE NOTEBOOK

Scientists classify millions of species.

Taxonomy is the science of classifying and naming organisms.

Classification is the process of arranging organisms in groups.

To classify organisms, scientists compare their characteristics.

organisms

seven levels

arrange into groups

CLASSIFICATION

Linnaeus

similar trait

systems can change

Scientists develop systems for classifying living things.

BEFORE, you learned

- Natural selection helps explain how new species develop
- Evidence indicates that species change over time
- New species develop from ancestral species

NOW, you will learn

- Why scientists classify living things
- That taxonomists study biological relationships
- About evidence used to classify organisms

VOCABULARY

classification p. 44
taxonomy p. 44

THINK ABOUT

How are these organisms similar?

Both a worm and a caterpillar share many characteristics. Both have long, skinny bodies that are divided into segments. But an earthworm moves underground, has no legs or eyes, and can grow back segments that are lost. A caterpillar crawls aboveground and is just one part of a butterfly's life cycle. As you read this chapter, think about whether you would classify these animals together or separately.

Scientists classify millions of species.

About 400 years ago, scientists who studied insects classified them based upon their appearance and behavior. If animals looked alike, researchers concluded that they were related. In the last few centuries scientists have realized that appearances can suggest false connections. Although caterpillars look like worms, they are actually an earlier stage of a butterfly's life.

For some people, the world seemed to grow larger during the 1600s. Travelers sailed to distant lands and oceans. Scientists went on many of these trips, observing and collecting samples of living things they had never seen before. In addition, the microscope allowed scientists to see tiny organisms that had been invisible before. But how could scientists organize and talk about this wonderful new knowledge?

Classification and Taxonomy

VOCABULARY

Add a description wheel for *classification* to your notebook. Include the word *group* in your diagram.

Two scientific processes deal with classifying and naming living things. **Classification** is the process of arranging organisms into groups based on similarities. **Taxonomy** is the science of naming and classifying organisms. A good system of classification allows you to organize a large amount of information so that it is easy to find and to understand. The system should provide a tool for comparing very large groups of organisms as well as smaller groups. Large groups might include all animals. Smaller groups might include birds, reptiles, or mammals.

A good system of taxonomy allows people to communicate about organisms. Before the 1700s, scientists had not agreed on a system of naming and grouping organisms. Take, for example, the common wild briar rose. Some scientists called it *Rosa sylvestris inodora seu canina* (odorless woodland dog rose). Others used the name *Rosa sylvestris alba cum rubore, folio glabro* (pinkish-white woodland rose with hairless leaves). Plus, any scientist studying a species could change the name.

These long Latin names may sound confusing, but even common names can be confusing. In England the bird called a robin—Britain's national bird—is only distantly related to the bird called a robin in the United States, even though they both have red feathers on their chests. A daddy longlegs could be either a long-legged relative of spiders (in the United States) or a long-legged relative of mosquitoes (in England).

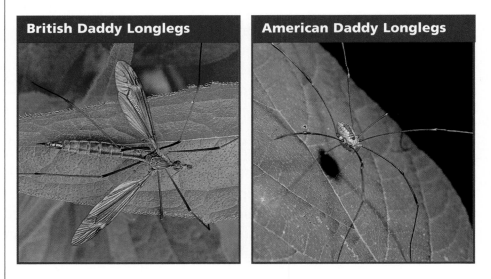

British Daddy Longlegs

American Daddy Longlegs

Clearly, biologists need both a system for organizing and a system for naming. Each name should refer to one specific type of organism. That way, scientists can use the species name and be sure that everybody knows exactly which organism they are talking about.

RESOURCE CENTER
CLASSZONE.COM

Find out more about taxonomy.

CHECK YOUR READING What is the difference between classification and taxonomy?

Using Classification

To classify organisms, scientists use similarities and differences among species. Sometimes these differences are easy to see, such as whether an animal has fur, feathers, or scales. Other times, seeing the differences requires special laboratory equipment, such as equipment to study DNA.

A classification system can help you identify unfamiliar organisms. For example, if you had never heard of a caracal but were told that it was a kind of cat, you already would know many things about it. It has fur, fangs, and sharp claws. It's a meat eater, not a plant eater. You would know these things because the caracal shares those characteristics with all of the members of the cat family.

If you looked up *caracal* in an encyclopedia, you'd find that your guesses were right. The caracal is a small wildcat native to Africa, the Middle East, and India. It weighs about 13 to 19 kilograms (29 to 42 pounds). The name *caracal* comes from a Turkish word meaning "black-eared."

The more characteristics two organisms share, the more similar their names should be in the classification system. The caracal, a pet cat, and all the cats below are different in size, habitat, and other characteristics. But they also have many similarities, and all belong to the cat family, Felidae.

Like other cats, a caracal has fur, sharp fangs, and is a meat eater.

Jaguars are muscular cats that may be over two meters long.

Ocelots are small hunters and tree climbers.

Some **lynx** have thick hair and live in colder climates.

READING VISUALS **COMPARE/CONTRAST:** What traits do these cats have in common?

Taxonomists study biological relationships.

READING TiP

Taxonomy, taxonomist, and *taxon* all share the same root.

Scientists need a simple, standard way of arranging all of the different species. The science of taxonomy is related to the Greek word *taxis,* which means "arrangement." Taxonomists are the scientists who classify and name organisms based on their similarities and differences. A taxon is a group of organisms that share certain traits. Taxons can be broad, like animals and plants, or more specific, like cats and roses.

As you learned in Chapter 1, living things evolve over time. A single species found in a fossil record might be the ancestor of many different species found on Earth today. Taxonomists study the relationships between species, trying to discover how one species evolved as compared with another species. Species that share ancestors are grouped together.

To determine how to classify organisms, scientists compare a variety of characteristics, or traits. A trait is a characteristic or behavior that can be used to tell two species apart, such as size or bone structure. If two organisms share a trait, taxonomists try to determine if they share the trait because they share an ancestor.

CHECK YOUR READING How do taxonomists use biological relationships to classify organisms?

INVESTIGATE Classifying Leaves

How can you classify leaves?

PROCEDURE

1. Decide, as a class, what traits you will use to classify leaves. You may use size, shape, color, vein patterns, texture, or anything else that you observe.

2. Work with a few classmates. Sort your leaves into four or five taxons, based on the characteristics chosen in step 1. Give each taxon a name that describes its common traits.

3. Compare your classification scheme with those of other groups.

WHAT DO YOU THINK?

- How did you arrange the leaves into groups?
- Did your methods of classifying leaves match those of other student groups?

CHALLENGE How does your group's classification scheme compare with the scheme scientists use for classification?

SKILL FOCUS
Classifying

MATERIALS
- leaves
- hand lens

TIME
20 minutes

Biological Relationships

Leafy Sea Dragon

The **sargassum fish** and the sea dragon are both fish with wavy fronds.

Both the **sea horse** and sea dragon have the same basic body shape.

This **sargassum seaweed** and the sea dragon both have leafy fronds.

Look at the photographs and try to determine to which organism a leafy sea dragon is more closely related. The leafy sea dragon shares traits with all of the other organisms pictured. For example, the sea dragon and the sargassum seaweed look similar, with greenish wavy fronds. But the sea dragon is an animal that moves, gets food from other organisms, and breathes oxygen. The sargassum seaweed is not an animal, it is a type of algae.

The sargassum fish shares more traits with the sea dragon, but its body is a much different shape and has scales. In fact, the leafy sea dragon is an animal that is closely related to a sea horse. Both have heads and bodies with similar shapes, and neither has scales. The sea horse shares more traits with the leafy sea dragon than with the other two organisms.

Taxonomists take evidence and try to reconstruct the evolution of a species. Then they place the species in the classification system. Scientists use physical evidence, such as fur, bones, and teeth. They also use genetic evidence, which is found within an organism's DNA.

Physical Evidence

Physical Evidence

Steller's Jay
• Lives only west of the Rocky Mountains
• Has a solid black head and neck and almost no white feathers

Blue Jay
• Lives mostly east of the Rocky Mountains
• Has blue, black, and white feathers on its wings and neck

The primary tools early scientists used for taxonomy were their eyes and measuring devices. They collected examples of organisms and noted characteristics, such as color, size, weight, and how groups of organisms obtain energy. Scientists who studied animals observed the internal structure, as well as outward appearances. These physical features are still important today.

Individuals of two species, such as the two jays shown to the left, can have many similarities as well as some differences. One obvious difference is the color pattern. Another is the area of the world in which they live. Blue jays live east of the Rocky Mountains, and steller's jays live west of the Rockies. The common names and the scientific names reflect the differences and the common ancestor: blue jay, *Cyanocitta cristata* and steller's jay, *Cyanocitta stelleri*.

Skeletons, shells, and other hard parts of organisms become fossilized more easily than soft parts do. Scientists can observe and measure fossilized bones or pieces of bones and compare them with each other. They can also compare bones of species that are extinct with bones of modern species. From such studies, scientists can determine many things about the organism. Physical evidence provides clues about how an organism may have lived, how it moved, or what type of food it ate.

All of this physical evidence helps scientists see that all living organisms are related by evolution. Some are more closely related than others. This means they share a more recent ancestor.

 CHECK YOUR READING How could comparing fossilized bones with a modern animal's bones help you see the modern animal's evolutionary history?

Genetic Evidence

In the early 20th century scientists discovered that organisms inherit their traits through structures called genes. In the mid-1950s they observed that genes are made of DNA and that DNA stores coded information.

Today scientists can use laboratory machines to catalog each component of an organism's DNA. With that information stored on a computer, scientists can compare the components of a gene from one organism with the components of the same gene from another organism.

Genetic evidence usually supports physical evidence, but not always. Consider the example shown on page 49. For years, taxonomists argued about how to classify this small, reddish animal from China. Its scientific name is *Ailurus fulgens*, and the common name is red panda.

Genetic Evidence

Both of these pandas live in the same habitat, have similar faces, and eat bamboo. But genetic evidence shows that red pandas and giant pandas are only distant relatives.

Red Panda

Giant Panda

Red pandas have more DNA in common with **raccoons.**

Giant pandas have more DNA in common with **spectacled bears.**

Racoon

Spectacled Bear

Later, scientists discovered a larger, bearlike animal in China, which they called the giant panda. Both pandas ate only bamboo, shared a common name, and their faces looked similar. Scientists concluded they were related to each other and to raccoons. However, molecular evidence has shown that the red panda is more closely related to raccoons and the giant panda is more closely related to bears.

2.1 Review

KEY CONCEPTS

1. Describe the benefits of classifying species.

2. Why do taxonomists study biological relationships?

3. How do scientists use genetic evidence when classifying organisms?

CRITICAL THINKING

4. **Analyze** Why do people need a universal system of naming organisms?

5. **Predict** The animal called a marbled godwit is a bird. What traits would you predict it has?

⬥ CHALLENGE

6. **Synthesize** Suppose you found two species of cave-dwelling lizards without eyes living on opposite sides of the world. Explain how you would try to determine if the two species were closely related.

MATH TUTORIAL
CLASSZONE.COM

Click on Math Tutorial for more help with percents and fractions.

Differences Between Species

Does it surprise you to learn that roughly 50 percent of the DNA in your cells is nearly identical to the DNA in the cells of a banana? You probably know from experience that 50 percent is the same as one half. But you can also convert any percent to a fraction by using the number 100 to represent the whole. Fifty parts out of 100 is the same as one half. Another example is shown below.

Example

Comparing the cells of two species, scientists find 40 percent of the DNA is identical. How can you show what fraction that is?

(1) Rewrite the percent as a numerator with a denominator of 100.

$$\frac{40}{100}$$

(2) Reduce the fraction. Use the greatest common factor (GCF) to write the numerator and the denominator as products.

$$\frac{40}{100} = \frac{2 \cdot 20}{5 \cdot 20}$$

(3) Divide the GCF by itself to get $\frac{1}{1}$, or 1.

$$\frac{2}{5} \cdot \frac{20}{20} = \frac{2}{5} \cdot 1 = \frac{2}{5}$$

ANSWER: 40 percent $= \frac{2}{5}$

Rewrite each sentence, changing the percent to a fraction.

1. About 85 percent of the DNA in human cells is similar to the DNA in mouse cells.

2. The tooth of a modern great white shark can be 34 percent of the length of a fossil tooth from a prehistoric shark.

3. There are about 20 percent as many penguin species as there are pine tree species in the world today.

4. There are about 8 percent as many bear species as pine tree species.

CHALLENGE Choose one example or exercise on this page. Tell whether the comparison works better as a fraction or a percent. Explain why.

2.2

Biologists use seven levels of classification.

◀ **BEFORE**, you learned

- Classification is a system of organization
- Evidence is used to classify organisms

▶ **NOW**, you will learn

- About scientific names
- About seven levels of classification
- How to use a dichotomous key

VOCABULARY

genus p. 52
binomial nomenclature p. 52
dichotomous key p. 56

EXPLORE Classification

What data do you need to identify objects?

PROCEDURE

① Have one student in your group think of a secret object. The student should then tell the group one characteristic (shape, color, size, type, and so on) of that object.

② The rest of the group guesses the object's identity. Each time someone guesses incorrectly, another characteristic of the object should be given. Record the characteristics and guesses as you go.

③ When the secret object is guessed correctly, begin again with a different student picking a different secret object.

WHAT DO YOU THINK?

- How many characteristics did it usually take to guess an object's identity?
- How does this exercise relate to identifying organisms?

Linnaeus named about 4000 species.

SUPPORTING MAIN IDEAS
Make a chart to show information that supports the first main idea presented: *Linnaeus named about 4000 species.*

Scientists name species and arrange them into groups. One scientist named Carolus Linnaeus developed systems for both naming species and organizing them into groups. All 4000 species that Linnaeus named were plants or animals. Today, scientists have named over a million species. Linnaeus used appearance to group species. As you have read, modern scientists also use appearance, along with other types of evidence, to arrange species into groups.

Naming Species

Sometimes using only one word to name an organism isn't specific enough. If you are telling a friend about your favorite writer, you might name Mary Oliver or Mary Whitebird or Mary Shelley. Using only "Mary" won't help your friend know the author you name, so you use two words. In a similar way, scientists use two words to name organisms.

A **genus** (JEE-nuhs) is a group of species that have similar characteristics. For example, the genus *Ursus* groups all of the animals known as bears. Included in this genus are *Ursus arctos* (grizzly bears), and *Ursus maritimus* (polar bears). Members of the same genus are closely related.

The system for naming species developed by Linnaeus is the basis of modern taxonomy. We call this system **binomial nomenclature** (by-NOH-mee-uhl NOH-muhn-KLAY-chuhr). *Binomial* means "two names" and *nomenclature* means "list of names." So binomial nomenclature describes a system of naming something using two names, or words. Most scientific names are Latin terms.

INVESTIGATE Binomial Nomenclature

How do you assign names?

PROCEDURE

1. Place ten objects on a table where everybody in the class can see them.

2. Give each object a genus name. Use a dictionary to come up with names that sound scientific. You may use only three genus names for the ten objects, so some names must apply to more than one objects.

3. Give each object a species name, using the dictionary again if you wish.

4. Write each object's full scientific name on an index card.

5. Trade your index cards with those of another group. Try to match their cards with the ten objects.

SKILL FOCUS
Classifying

MATERIALS
- objects
- dictionary
- 10 index cards

TIME
30 minutes

WHAT DO YOU THINK?

- How did the other group arrange the objects into genus names? How was their arrangement different from your group's?

- Why is it important for the names to be as descriptive as possible?

CHALLENGE Repeat the exercise, but now give each object a one-word name. Does this limitation make coming up with names easier or harder?

Binomial Nomenclature

All organisms are given a unique two-part name. Some organisms have the same species names: *gracilis* means "slender" or "graceful." Without the genus name, the species name is unclear.

Aubrieta gracilis
(false rockcress)

Chameleo gracilis
(gracile chameleon)

Mammillaria gracilis
(thimble cactus)

Using Scientific Names

Linnaeus's system of binomial nomenclature made communication about certain species much easier. When naming an organism, the use of a genus name as well as a species name is necessary.

If the genus name is not included in the scientific name, the identity of a species can be a mystery. For example, the species name of the three different species shown above is *gracilis*. The word *gracilis* means "graceful" or "slender" in Latin.

- *Aubrieta gracilis* is a type of flower found in a rock garden.
- *Chameleo gracilis* is a type of lizard called a chameleon.
- *Mammillaria gracilis* is a type of cactus.

People follow certain rules when they write scientific names. The genus name comes first; the first letter is capitalized and the entire name is in italics. The species name is also written in italics, it follows the genus name, and the first letter is lowercased.

 CHECK YOUR READING What is the difference between a genus and a species?

In addition to species and genus, the classification system includes several larger groups. Each larger group includes one or more smaller groups. Turn to page 54 to read about the larger groups in our modern system of classification.

Organisms can be classified into seven levels.

SUPPORTING MAIN IDEAS
Make a chart to show information that supports the main idea that *organisms can be classified into seven levels.*

READING TiP

Phyla is the plural form of *phylum.*

You've read about species and genus, the most specific levels of the classification system most scientists use today. There are seven levels that describe a species. The largest level is the kingdom, the group containing the most species. The seven levels of classification for a spotted turtle and a housecat are listed below.

1. Kingdom (Animalia—the animals)
2. Phylum (Chordata—animals with backbones)
3. Class (Mammalia—mammals, or furry animals that nurse their young)
4. Order (Carnivora—carnivores, or animals that kill and eat other animals)
5. Family (Felidae—the cat family)
6. Genus (*Felis*—housecats, cougars, and many others)
7. Species (*catus*—all housecats, no matter what their breed)

Like the cat, the turtle is also classified into seven levels. However, only the two largest levels, Animalia and Chordata, are the same as the classification for a housecat. The more names an organism shares with another organism, the more closely related the two organisms are. Cats and turtles are both animals with backbones, but are otherwise different. Spotted turtles have more traits in common with snakes and lizards than with cats. Lizards, snakes, and turtles all belong in the class Reptilia. Phyla are more specific than kingdoms, classes are more specific than phyla, and so on. The illustration on page 55 shows how kingdom is the broadest grouping of organisms, and species is the most specific.

Clemmys guttata

Classification Hierarchy		
	Spotted turtle	Cat
Kingdom	Animalia	Animalia
Phylum	Chordata	Chordata
Class	Reptilia	Mammalia
Order	Testudines	Carnivora
Family	Emydidae	Felidae
Genus	*Clemmys*	*Felis*
Species	*guttata*	*catus*

Felis catus

Classifying Organisms

Moving from kingdom to species, each level includes a smaller set of organisms.

1 Kingdom
Animalia:
Animals

2 Phylum
Chordata:
With backbone or
similar structure

3 Class
Reptilia:
Reptiles

4 Order
Testudines:
Turtles

5 Family
Emydidae:
Water turtles

6 Genus
Clemmys:
North American
pond turtles

7 Species
guttata:
Spotted turtle

Spotted turtle
Clemmys guttata

Scientists can compare very broad categories of organisms, such as kingdoms and phyla. Or they can compare very specific categories, such as species. If scientists wish to compare all the different types of turtles to one another, then they will compare the organisms in the order Testudines. But if scientists want to compare turtles that live in or near water, then they will compare only organisms in the family Emydidae.

You can remember the classification levels and their order with this memory aid: Kings Play Chess On Fat Green Stools. The first letter of each word is the same as the first letter in each level of classification: *kingdom, phylum, class, order, family, genus,* and *species.* A complete classification of humans goes like this: kingdom Animalia, phylum Chordata, class Mammalia, order Primates, family Hominidae, genus *Homo,* species *sapiens.*

 CHECK YOUR READING Which level of classification in the seven-level system includes the most species?

Dichotomous keys and field guides help people identify organisms.

With millions of organisms on Earth, how could a specific one be identified? Even if you know some of the larger categories, it can be difficult to find the species, genus, or even family name of many organisms from a long list of possibilities.

Take a beetle, for example. Even if you knew that it is in the kingdom Animalia, phylum Arthropoda (animals with jointed legs), class Insecta (insects), and order Coleoptera (hard-winged insects), you'd still have to choose among 300,000 known species of beetles that have been discovered around the world.

READING TiP
The prefix *di-* means "two."

Taxonomists have come up with a tool to identify organisms such as this beetle. A **dichotomous key** (dy-KAHT-uh-muhs) asks a series of questions that can be answered in only two ways. Your answer to each question leads you to another question with only two choices. After a number of such questions, you will identify the organism. One example of a dichotomous key for trees is shown on page 57.

The questions in a dichotomous key gradually narrow down the list of possible organisms. The questions can ask about any trait. The idea is simply to make identifying an organism as easy as possible. The dichotomous key for trees, for example, asks a set of questions that only ask about the traits of the leaves. Leaves are usually easy to get from a tree that needs to be identified, and they include many characteristics that can be used to tell different trees apart.

SIMULATION CLASSZONE.COM

Use an interactive dichotomous key.

Dichotomous Key

Use the dichotomous key below to discover on what tree the circled leaf is found.

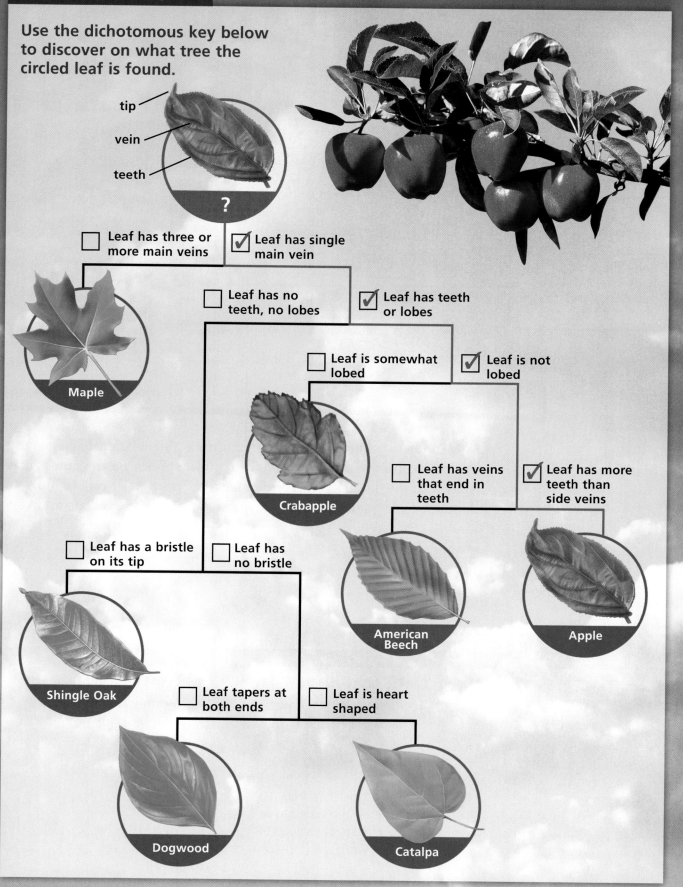

tip

vein

teeth

?

☐ **Leaf has three or more main veins**

☑ **Leaf has single main vein**

Maple

☐ **Leaf has no teeth, no lobes**

☑ **Leaf has teeth or lobes**

☐ **Leaf is somewhat lobed**

☑ **Leaf is not lobed**

Crabapple

☐ **Leaf has veins that end in teeth**

☑ **Leaf has more teeth than side veins**

☐ **Leaf has a bristle on its tip**

☐ **Leaf has no bristle**

American Beech

Apple

Shingle Oak

☐ **Leaf tapers at both ends**

☐ **Leaf is heart shaped**

Dogwood

Catalpa

A bird's **scientific name** is shown next to its common name. The first name is the genus, and the second name is the species.

Range maps show where a bird can be found in each season.

Body shape and body size give clues to determining if you have identified the right bird.

[Field guide page contents:]

NEW WORLD VULTURES. Family Cathartidae.
Blackish, eaglelike birds often seen soaring high in wide circles. Their naked heads are relatively smaller than those of hawks and eagles. Often incorrectly called buzzards. Sexes alike. **FOOD:** Carrion. **RANGE:** S. Canada to Cape Horn. **NO. OF SPECIES:** World, 7; East, 2.

TURKEY VULTURE *Cathartes aura* Common
26–32" (66–82 cm) Nearly eagle-sized (wingspread 6 ft.). When overhead, note two-toned wings (dark coverts, silver flight feathers). Soars with wings in a slight dihedral (a shallow V) rocking and tilting unsteadily. At close range, small naked *red head* of adult is evident; immature bird has dark head (like a Black Vulture). **RANGE:** S. Canada to Cape Horn. Migratory in north. **HABITAT:** Usually seen soaring in the sky or perched on dead trees or posts, at carrion, or on the ground sunning with wings outstretched.

BLACK VULTURE *Coragyps atratus* Common
23–27" (58–68 cm) Wingspan under 5 ft. This large blackish scavenger is readily identified by the short tail that barely projects from rear edge of wings and by a silver patch restricted to outer wing. Pale feet sometimes project beyond tail. Note quick shallow flapping flight alternating with short glides. **SIMILAR SPECIES:** Turkey Vulture has a longer tail; flaps less, soars unsteadily with a rocking motion. *Caution:* Young Turkey Vulture has dark head. **RANGE:** Cen. and e. U.S. to n. Chile, n. Argentina. Range is extending north. **HABITAT:** Similar to Turkey Vulture's.

KING VULTURE *Sarcoramphus papa*
32" (80 cm) A whitish vulture with black flight feathers, gaudy head and neck. A rare resident of tropical America. Recorded by John and William Bartram on St. Johns R. in Fla. in 1765–1766, but this species has not been seen in the U.S. since.

CARACARAS AND FALCONS. Family Falconidae.

CARACARAS. Subfamily Caracarinae.
Large, long-legged birds of prey with naked faces. Sexes alike. **FOOD:** Our only U.S. species eats chiefly carrion and insects. **RANGE:** S. U.S. to Tierra del Fuego, Falklands. **NO. OF SPECIES:** World, 10; East, 1.

CRESTED CARACARA *Caracara cheriway* Fairly common, restricted
20–25" (50–63 cm) A large, long-legged, big-headed, dark bird of prey often seen feeding with vultures or hunting on foot in pasturelands. Its black crest and red face are distinctive. In flight, its underbody presents alternating areas of light and dark; white chest, black belly, and whitish, dark-tipped tail. Note combination of *pale* wing patch and white chest. Young bird is browner, streaked below. **RANGE:** Sw. U.S., Tex., and Fla. to S. America. **HABITAT:** Prairies, rangeland, desert.

92 PLATES

SCAVENGERS

TURKEY VULTURE
adult
immature

BLACK VULTURE
adult

above, King Vulture
(formerly in Florida)

CRESTED CARACARA
immature
adult

Another tool for identifying organisms is a field guide. Field guides include paintings or photographs of familiar species. Flower guides may start with the flower's color. Bird guides are arranged by orders and families. Field guides also include maps showing where organisms live.

CHECK YOUR READING What two tools have taxonomists developed to identify organisms?

2.2 Review

KEY CONCEPTS

1. What is binomial nomenclature?

2. Write the names of the seven levels of classification. Which level contains the most organisms?

3. What makes a dichotomous key easy to use?

CRITICAL THINKING

4. **Summarize** What were Carolus Linnaeus's main contributions to taxonomy?

5. **Compare and Contrast** Compare a dichotomous key with a typical field guide. What are the strengths and weaknesses of each?

CHALLENGE

6. **Synthesize** Predict what differences you might find among organisms in the same species.

The Undiscovered

Everyone agrees that insects are the largest group of animals on Earth, but nobody knows exactly how many insect species exist. Some estimates predict that there are as many as 30 million. However, only about 900,000 have been classified. Twenty-nine million insect species may be waiting to be discovered!

Where in the World?

Many of the new insect species are found in tropical forests of South America and Asia. But plenty may be hiding close to your own home.

- The most massive bug in Southern California went undiscovered until April 4, 2002. This wingless relative of the Jerusalem cricket looks something like a puffed-up 3-inch-long ant.

- While studying for her graduate degree, Christina Sandoval captured insects in Santa Barbara, California. She caught an unidentified species of walking stick insect, which she named after herself: *Timema cristinae*.

- The Hanford Nuclear Reservation, in Washington state, was closed to the public for about 50 years. After it opened for cleanup, the Nature Conservancy found 27 new insect species in just 4 years, including a new micromoth less than 1/8 inch long.

Scientists think that over one third of the estimated 164,000 insect species in the United States have yet to be discovered and named. Start looking. Who knows where they'll be!

A Whole New Order

In March 2002, for the first time in 87 years, a whole new order of insects was discovered. Insects in this order look like a cross between stick insects, praying mantises, and grasshoppers. Upon its discovery, the order was nicknamed *gladiators*. Now called *Mantophasmatodea*, the "gladiator bugs" raised the total number of insect orders to 31.

EXPLORE

1. **ANALYZE** List some things about an insect that could be included in its species name. Tell why each is important.

2. **CHALLENGE** Scientists recently discovered a new centipede in New York's Central Park, the first new species in the park in over 100 years. Centipedes are related to insects. Find out what centipedes and insects have in common and how they differ.

RESOURCE CENTER
CLASSZONE.COM
Learn more about newly discovered insects.

An adult Jerusalem cricket can reach 2 inches in length.

Classification systems change as scientists learn more.

◀ BEFORE, you learned	▶ NOW, you will learn
• Scientists give each species a unique scientific name	• About the connection between new discoveries and taxonomy
• There are seven levels of classification	• About three domains
• Dichotomous keys help us identify organisms	• About six kingdoms

VOCABULARY

domain p. 61
Plantae p. 63
Animalia p. 63
Protista p. 63
Fungi p .63
Archaea p. 63
Bacteria p. 63

THINK ABOUT

How do scientists define kingdoms?

Look at this photograph of a sea urchin. It lives its life buried in or slowly moving across the ocean floor. The sea urchin's mouth is located on its under-side. It feeds on food particles that settle on or are buried in

the ocean floor. The sea urchin doesn't appear to have much in common with a tiger, an alligator, even a human. Yet all of these organisms belong in the same kingdom, called Animalia. Why do you think scientists would group these organisms together?

Taxonomy changes as scientists make discoveries.

The list of species continues to grow as scientists discover new species. In addition, taxonomists are learning more about the evolutionary history of species. As you read in Section 2.1, new knowledge resulted in the reclassification of species such as the giant panda. Both the names of species and the groups into which they are arranged may change as a result of discoveries about the evolution of these species.

Early scientists described two large groups of organisms—plants and animals. Plants were described as green and nonmoving. Animals moved. Most scientists today use a system that includes six kingdoms. In addition, taxonomists have added a level of organization above the kingdom level.

Three Domains

Microscopes and other advances in technology have allowed scientists to observe that there are three fundamentally different types of cells. On the basis of this observation, scientists have arranged kingdoms into larger groups called **domains.** For example, the domain Eukarya contains the protists, fungi, plants, and animals.

RESOURCE CENTER
CLASSZONE.COM
Find out more about modern classification.

The table below summarizes the relationships among the six kingdoms and the three domains. You will learn more about kingdoms in the rest of this section.

Domains and Kingdoms

Domain	Bacteria	Archaea	Eukarya			
Kingdom	Bacteria	Archaea	Protista	Fungi	Plantae	Animalia
Cell type	No nucleus	No nucleus	With nucleus	With nucleus	With nucleus	With nucleus
Cell number	Unicellular	Unicellular	Unicellular	Mostly multicellular	Multicellular	Multicellular
How organisms get energy	Varies	Varies	Varies	Absorbs materials	Uses sunlight	Consumes food

The photographs below show examples of cells from each domain. One of the traits that distinguishes cells of Eukarya from cells of Bacteria and Archaea is the presence of a nucleus. Cells that contain a nucleus are called eukaryotic cells, and cells that do not contain a nucleus are called prokaryotic cells. The domains Bacteria and Archaea include only organisms with prokaryotic cells. The domain Eukarya includes only organisms with eukaryotic cells.

 CHECK YOUR READING How are prokaryotic cells different from eukaryotic cells?

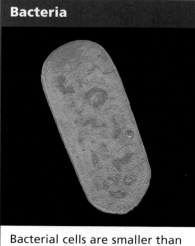

Bacteria

Bacterial cells are smaller than Eukarya cells and have no nucleus.

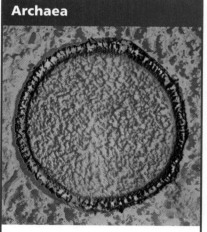

Archaea

Archaea cells have a distinctive chemistry and can survive extreme environments.

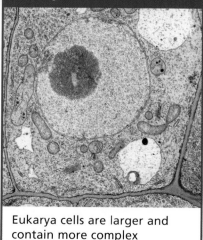

Eukarya

Eukarya cells are larger and contain more complex structures.

All living things on Earth can be classified in six kingdoms.

Plantae
- Plants are multicellular and live on land.
- Plants obtain energy from sunlight.
- A plant cell has a nucleus, a cell wall, and chloroplasts.

Animalia
- Animals are multicellular and able to move.
- Animals obtain energy by eating food.
- An animal cell has a nucleus but no cell wall or chloroplasts.

Protista
- Most protists are single-celled.
- Multicellular protists lack complex structure.
- A protist cell has a nucleus.

Fungi
- All fungi except yeasts are multicellular.
- Fungi obtain energy by absorbing materials.
- A fungus cell has a nucleus and a cell wall, but no chloroplasts.

Archaea
- Archaea are unicellular organisms without nuclei.
- Archaea cells have different chemicals than bacteria.
- Archaea can live in extreme conditions.

Bacteria
- Bacteria are unicellular organisms.
- A bacterial cell has no nucleus.
- Bacteria reproduce by dividing in two.

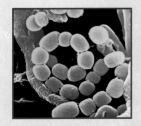

Six Kingdoms

The classification system that many scientists use today has six kingdoms. Every known species on Earth is included in one of these six kingdoms.

- Kingdom **Plantae** (PLAN-TEE) includes plants such as trees, grass, and moss.

- Kingdom **Animalia** (AN-uh-MAL-yuh) includes animals, from lions and tigers and bears to bugs and multicellular microbes.

- Kingdom **Protista** (pruh-TIHS-tuh) includes organisms that don't fit easily into animals, plants, or fungi. They are either unicellular organisms or have a simple multicellular structure.

- Kingdom **Fungi** (FUHN-jy) includes mushrooms, molds, and yeasts.

- Kingdom **Archaea** (AHR-kee-uh) contains organisms that are similar to bacteria, but have a cell structure that is so different that scientists separate them into their own kingdom.

- Kingdom **Bacteria** (bak-TIHR-ee-uh) are unicellular organisms with no nucleus.

This system may change as scientists learn more about the species in each kingdom. Before 1990, most scientists preferred a five-kingdom system that combined Archaea and Bacteria into a single kingdom. However, as scientists learned of chemical differences between the cells of the species, they arranged them into two kingdoms. Today, some scientists suggest that the kingdom Protista should be arranged into smaller kingdoms because of the many differences among its species. Many scientists agree on a three domain and six kingdom system similar to the one summarized on pages 61–63.

CHECK YOUR READING Which of the six kingdoms include unicellular organisms?

VOCABULARY
Add description wheels for *Plantae, Animalia, Protista, Fungi, Archaea,* and *Bacteria* to your notebook. You may want to add to your diagrams as you read the section.

The two most familiar kingdoms are plants and animals.

Carolus Linnaeus divided all of the species he identified into two large groups: plants and animals. People still use these groups to describe most living things today. But these two kingdoms also include unfamiliar organisms.

It might seem odd that living things that are so different from each other—humans, elephants, termites, ducks, fish, worms—are all part of the same group. However, all of these organisms share some general traits, just as all plants share another set of general traits.

Plantae

About 250,000 plant species live on Earth. They range from tiny mosses to the largest organisms on the planet, giant sequoia trees. The oldest living organism on our planet is a plant called the bristlecone pine. Some living bristlecone pines were growing when the Egyptians built the pyramids, about 4000 years ago.

All plants are multicellular and are eukaryotes, which means their DNA is stored in the nucleus of their cells. All plants are able to make sugars using the Sun's energy. Plants cannot move from place to place, but they can grow around objects, turn toward light, and grow upward. Plant cells are different from animal cells, because plant cells have tough walls outside their cell membranes.

Clematis viticella
(Italian clematis)

 ## Animalia

Scientists have already named a million species in the kingdom Animalia. Many different types of animals inhabit the planet, but more than 90 percent of the named species are insects. The animal kingdom also includes familiar animals such as whales, sharks, humans, bears, dogs, and fish.

All animals get their energy by eating other organisms or by eating food made by other organisms. Animals have the ability to move around for at least part of their life. Most animals have mouths and some type of nervous system. Plant and animal cells are both eukaryotic, but animal cells have no cell walls.

CHECK YOUR READING What is the most abundant type of species in the animal kingdom?

Abracadabrella birdsville
(jumping spider)

Giraffa camelopardalis
(giraffe)

Octopus cyanea
(day octopus)

Other organisms make up four more kingdoms.

Carolus Linnaeus's classification systems included the organisms he knew about in the late 1700s. Some of the organisms Linnaeus called plants—the mushrooms, molds, and their relatives—turned out to have some characteristics very different from those of plants. Biologists now put fungi in a kingdom of their own.

Three other kingdoms consist mainly of microscopic organisms. These are Protista, Archaea, and Bacteria. Most organisms on Earth are classified as bacteria or archaea. These are prokaryotic organisms, which have small, simple cells and no nuclei.

CHECK YOUR READING What are the four kingdoms besides Plantae and Animalia?

Protista

The kingdom Protista includes a wide variety of organisms. Most protists are unicellular. Protists that are multicellular have structures that are too simple to be classified as animals, plants, or fungi. All protists have large, complex cells with a true nucleus (eukaryotes). Some eat other organisms as animals do; some get energy from sunlight as plants do. Some protists resemble fungi. However, protists that are multicellular do not have as many specialized cells or structures as plants, animals, and fungi.

Many protists live in pond water or sea water. The largest of the unicellular species are barely visible without a microscope. However, large organisms such as seaweeds are also classified as Protista. Some seaweeds can grow hundreds of feet in a single year.

Different groups of protists evolved from different ancestors. Scientists still debate whether kingdom Protista should be classified as one kingdom or should be split into several kingdoms.

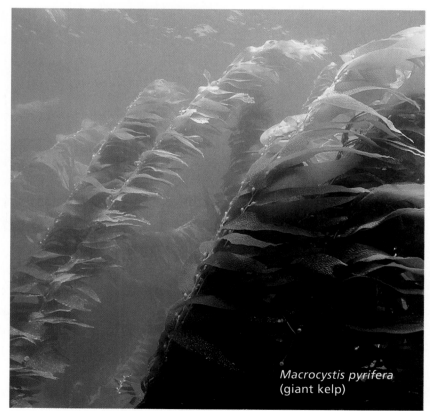

Macrocystis pyrifera (giant kelp)

Fungi

Every time a loaf of bread is baked, a fungus is responsible for the rising dough. One group of fungi called yeasts makes it possible for us to make bread and many other food products. Another type of fungi that people eat includes some mushrooms. A mushroom grows in thin threads underground, and only the small cap breaks above the ground.

READING TiP

Fungi is the plural form of *fungus*.

Fungi are usually divided into three categories: mushrooms, molds, and yeasts. The trait that separates fungi from other organisms is that fungi take in nutrients from their surroundings instead of eating other organisms or using sunlight. Both plants and fungi remain rooted in one place. Most fungi have cell walls similar to the cell walls of plants. Unlike plants, however, many fungi act as decomposers, breaking down dead or decaying material into simpler parts that can be absorbed or recycled by other organisms.

Penicillium (bread mold)

Lepiota procera (parasol mushroom)

Archaea

In the mid-1990s a researcher studying the genes of some bacteria discovered that although they resembled bacteria in size and cell type, some species had very specific genetic differences. After more study, scientists decided to call these organisms archaea. They differ so much that scientists now classify archaea in the separate kingdom or domain of Archaea.

In some ways, archaea appear to be more related to eukaryotes—organisms with complex cells containing nuclei—than to bacteria. Archaea do not have nuclei, but their cell structure is different from that of bacteria. Like bacteria, archaea live in many environments, especially in the ocean. But they also live in some very extreme environments, such as boiling mud near geysers, hot vents at the bottom of the ocean, salty ponds, and deep under the sand.

Methanococcoides burtonii

 CHECK YOUR READING Which traits classify an organism as part of the kingdom Archaea?

Bacteria

Bacteria live nearly everywhere on Earth. This kingdom includes organisms that cause human disease and spoil food, but most of these organisms are helpful members of biological communities.

All bacteria are unicellular organisms. They have small, simple cells without a nucleus. Most bacteria have a cell wall outside the cell membrane, but this wall is not the same as the cell wall of plants. Bacteria reproduce by dividing in two, and can produce many new generations in a short period of time.

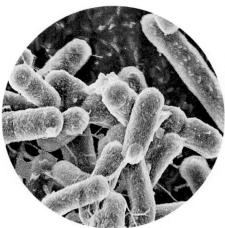

*Escherichia coli
(E. coli)*

Species and environments change.

In the last chapter you read about the ways species change over time. You have also read how the evolutionary history of species helps scientists classify living things.

Scientists have named over a million species and placed them into six kingdoms. In addition, scientists estimate that there are millions—maybe tens of millions—more species that haven't been discovered. Scientists have also discovered forms of life preserved in the fossil record. Some of those organisms are the ancestors of organisms that live today.

Species evolve over time as individual organisms and environments change. Individual organisms are faced with many other pressures that affect daily lives. These pressures may come from changes in their living space, in the availability of food or other resources, or from other organisms. In the next chapter, you will read about how groups of species are affected by changes in their surroundings.

2.3 Review

KEY CONCEPTS

1. What are the names of the six kingdoms used in the classification system?

2. How are species sorted into the various kingdoms?

CRITICAL THINKING

3. **Communicate** Make a table with columns headed Characteristics, Animalia, and Plantae. Using as many rows as needed, list characteristics that differ between these two kingdoms.

4. **Analyze** Explain how fungi differ from plants.

○ CHALLENGE

5. **Analyze** One bacterium has a membrane surrounding its DNA. Should this organism be classified with the eukaryotes? Why or why not?

CHAPTER INVESTIGATION

Making a Field Guide

OVERVIEW AND PURPOSE A field guide is an illustrated book that shows the differences and similarities among plant or animal organisms. In this activity you will
- observe and classify leaves
- prepare a field guide based on your observations

▶ Question

A field guide helps scientists identify organisms. Can you successfully prepare such a field guide? What would you like to know about how field guides are used and made? Write a question that begins with *Which, How, Why, When,* or *What.*

▶ Procedure

MATERIALS
- plastic gloves
- shoebox
- hand lens
- pencil
- paper
- tracing paper
- crayons

1. Make 5 or more tables like the one shown on the sample science notebook on page 69. Gather at least 5 samples of different leaves from an area that your teacher chooses. **CAUTION: Wear protective gloves when handling plants. Be aware of any poisonous plants in your area. Place your samples in a shoebox and bring them back to the classroom for observation.**

2. **CAUTION: Wear plastic gloves when handling leaf samples.** Use the hand lens to study the leaves that you gathered. Make a sketch of each of the leaves. Create leaf rubbings by placing each leaf between two sheets of tracing paper and rubbing the top paper with the side of a pencil or crayon. Record your observations about each leaf in one of the data tables.

step 2

3 Use the information in your table to prepare your field guide. Start by dividing your leaves into two groups on the basis of one of the characteristics you observed. Then compare the leaves in each group. How are they similar or different? Continue to observe and divide the samples in each group until each leaf is in a classification by itself.

4 Use scientific field guides or other sources to identify your sample leaves. Find out the common and scientific name for each leaf and add that information to your table.

5 Describe the location of each sample and what effect the plant it represents has on its environment. For example, does the plant provide food or shelter for animals? Does it have a commercial use, or is it an important part of the environment?

6 Use your data tables, sketches, and leaf rubbings to prepare your field guide for the chosen area.

▶ Observe and Analyze Write It Up

1. **CLASSIFY** What characteristics did you choose for classifying your leaf samples? Explain why you grouped the leaves the way you did.

2. **ANALYZE** Which characteristics of the leaves you gathered were most useful in finding their scientific names and in identifying them?

▶ Conclude — Write It Up

1. **INFER** Could you use the same characteristics you used to group your samples to classify leaves of other species?

2. **LIMITATIONS** Were there any leaves you could not classify? What would help you classify them?

3. **APPLY** How are field guides useful to scientists working on environmental studies? How are field guides useful to tourists or others who are exploring an environment?

▶ INVESTIGATE Further

CHALLENGE Combine your field guide with those made by all the other members of your class to make one large field guide. Use all the sketches and observations to classify leaves into several large groups.

Making a Field Guide: Leaf 1

Characteristic	Observations
Simple leaf or several leaflets	
Number of lobes	
Texture	
Leaf edge	
Vein patterns	

Common name
_____

Scientific name
_____

Location where found
_____

Uses/role in environment
_____

the BIG idea

Scientists have developed a system for classifying the great diversity of living things.

CONTENT REVIEW
CLASSZONE.COM

KEY CONCEPTS SUMMARY

2.1 Scientists develop systems for classifying living things.

- Living things are arranged in groups based on similarities.
- Classification is the process of arranging organisms into groups.
- Taxonomy involves classifying as well as naming species.

VOCABULARY
classification p. 44
taxonomy p. 44

2.2 Biologists use seven levels of classification.

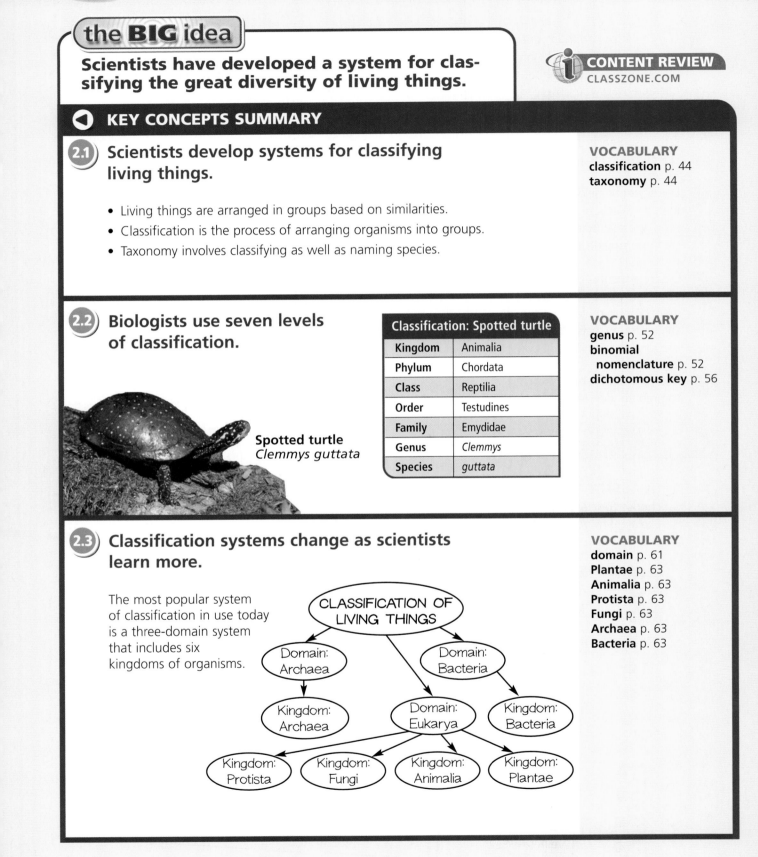

Spotted turtle
Clemmys guttata

Classification: Spotted turtle	
Kingdom	Animalia
Phylum	Chordata
Class	Reptilia
Order	Testudines
Family	Emydidae
Genus	*Clemmys*
Species	*guttata*

VOCABULARY
genus p. 52
binomial
  nomenclature p. 52
dichotomous key p. 56

2.3 Classification systems change as scientists learn more.

The most popular system of classification in use today is a three-domain system that includes six kingdoms of organisms.

CLASSIFICATION OF LIVING THINGS

Domain: Archaea → Kingdom: Archaea

Domain: Bacteria → Kingdom: Bacteria

Domain: Eukarya → Kingdom: Protista, Kingdom: Fungi, Kingdom: Animalia, Kingdom: Plantae

VOCABULARY
domain p. 61
Plantae p. 63
Animalia p. 63
Protista p. 63
Fungi p. 63
Archaea p. 63
Bacteria p. 63

Reviewing Vocabulary

Make a frame like the one shown for each vocabulary word listed below. Write the word in the center. Decide what information to frame it with. Use definitions, examples, descriptions, parts, or pictures.

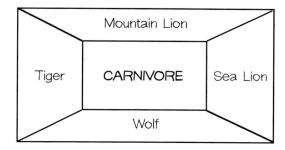

Mountain Lion

Tiger | CARNIVORE | Sea Lion

Wolf

1. Plantae

2. Animalia

3. Protista

4. Fungi

Reviewing Key Concepts

Multiple Choice *Choose the letter of the best answer.*

5. The scientific process of arranging organisms into groups based on similarities is
a. observation
b. classification
c. binomial nomenclature
d. dichotomy

6. The system of naming organisms developed by Carolus Linnaeus is called
a. binomial nomenclature
b. taxonomy
c. dichotomous nomenclature
d. classification

7. Which group includes the most species?
a. kingdom
b. family
c. domain
d. phylum

8. The science of taxonomy allows scientists to
a. identify unfamiliar organisms
b. classify and name organisms
c. refer to one specific type of organism
d. determine similar traits of organisms

9. Which allows scientists to use genetic information to classify organisms?
a. physical traits
b. DNA
c. fossil evidence
d. habitats

10. A dichotomous key contains a series of questions that people use to
a. find similar organisms
b. identify organisms
c. name organisms
d. describe organisms

11. What are the names of the three domains?
a. Plantae, Animalia, Protista
b. Bacteria, Protista, Fungi
c. Bacteria, Archaea, Eukarya
d. Protista, Archaea, Eukarya

12. Which is an example of a trait?
a. bone structure
b. DNA information
c. fossil records
d. habitat

13. A group of species that have similar characteristics is called
a. an order
b. a family
c. a phylum
d. a genus

14. Which characteristic is common to animals, plants, protists, and fungi?
a. ability to make their own food
b. eukaryotic cells
c. ability to move
d. multicellular structure

Short Answer *Write a short answer to each question.*

15. What are the rules for creating a scientific name for an organism?

16. How is a field guide different from a dichotomous key?

17. What types of information caused scientists to add the level of domain to the system of classification?

Thinking Critically

18. ANALYZE How do scientists use fossils to classify organisms?

19. APPLY Scientists once classified American vultures and African vultures together in the falcon family. Now, scientists know that American vultures are more closely related to storks. What type of evidence might scientists have used to come to this conclusion? Explain your answer.

20. EVALUATE Which two of these species are more closely related: *Felis catus, Felis concolor, Picea concolor?* How do you know?

21. INFER A scientist is studying the following organisms. What conclusions can you draw about the organisms based on their scientific names?

- *Ursus americanus*
- *Ursus arctos*
- *Ursus maritimus*

22. ANALYZE Two organisms you are studying are in the same class, but in a different order. What does this information tell you about the two organisms?

23. RANK Which of these have more groups of organisms: phylum or family? Explain your answer.

24. SUMMARIZE Describe how you would use a dichotomous key to identify this leaf.

25. SYNTHESIZE Why was it necessary for scientists to create groups for classifying organisms other than the groups of plants and animals described by Linnaeus?

26. CLASSIFY Suppose you discover a new organism that is single celled, has a nucleus, lives in the water, and uses sunlight to produce its energy. In which kingdom would you classify this organism? Explain.

the BIG idea

27. INFER Look again at the picture on pages 40–41. Now that you have finished the chapter, how would you change or add details to your answer to the question on the photograph?

28. PROVIDE EXAMPLES Imagine that you are a scientist studying a variety of organisms in a South American rain forest. You have classified one organism in the kingdom Animalia and another organism in the kingdom Plantae. Give examples of the characteristics that would enable you to classify each organism in those kingdoms.

UNIT PROJECTS

Check your schedule for your unit project. How are you doing? Be sure that you've placed data or notes from your research in your project folder.

Standardized Test Practice

For practice on your state test, go to . . .

TEST PRACTICE
CLASSZONE.COM

Analyzing Graphics

Choose the letter of the best response.

By following the steps in this chart, it is possible to find the type of tree to which a leaf belongs.

Step 1
1a) Leaves are needlelike.................Go to step 2
1b) Leaves are flat and scalelike.........Go to step 5

Step 2
2a) Needles are clustered...................Go to step 3
2b) Needles are not clustered..............Go to step 4

Step 3
3a) Clusters of 2–5 needles................Pine
3b) Clusters greater than 10.............Go to step 4

Step 4
4a) Needles soft................................Larch
4b) Needles stiff...............................True cedar

Step 5
5a) Needles are short and sharp........Giant sequoia
5b) Some needles are not sharp..........Go to Step 6

1. Which has leaves with clusters of 2–5 needles?
   a. pine tree
   b. larch tree
   c. true cedar tree
   d. giant sequoia

2. If a tree has clusters of needles greater than 10, you would go to
   a. step 1
   b. step 2
   c. step 3
   d. step 4

3. Each step on the key compares two
   a. species
   b. animals
   c. traits
   d. trees

4. A tree with soft needles that are not clustered is most likely a
   a. pine tree
   b. larch tree
   c. true cedar tree
   d. giant sequoia

5. Which statement best describes the characteristics of a giant sequoia?
   a. flat, scalelike needles that are short and sharp
   b. flat, scalelike needles that are stiff
   c. clustered needles that are soft
   d. clustered needles that are short and sharp

Extended Response

6. A biologist has discovered and collected a number of unknown plant species from a rain-forest environment. Explain what type of evidence a biologist would rely on to determine if the plant species were new. Give specific examples of what a biologist would look for. What process would scientists go through to name the new species?

7. As you learned in the chapter, there are scientists who classify and name organisms. Explain why it is important for these taxonomists to study biological relationships. What may these relationships indicate about early life and modern life?

TIMELINES in Science

LIFE Unearthed

How do scientists know about life on Earth millions of years ago? They dig, scratch, and hunt. The best clues they find are hidden in layers of rock. The rock-locked clues, called fossils, are traces or remains of living things from long ago. Some fossils show the actual bodies of organisms, while others, such as footprints, reveal behavior.

Before 1820, most fossil finds revealed the bodies of ocean life. Then large bones of lizardlike walking animals began turning up, and pictures of a new "terrible lizard," or dinosaur, took shape. Later, discoveries of tracks and nests showed behaviors such as flocking and caring for young. Even today, discoveries of "living fossils," modern relatives of prehistoric species, have offered us a rare glimpse of the activity of early life.

1824

Giant Lizards from Fragments

William Buckland describes *Megalosaurus*, a giant crocodilelike animal he studies from only a few bits of jaw, teeth, ribs, pelvis, and one leg. A year later Gideon Mantell assembles *Iguanodon*, a similar animal, from fossil bones.

EVENTS

1800	1810	1820

APPLICATIONS AND TECHNOLOGY

TECHNOLOGY

Removing Fossils with Care

The technology for removing fossils from rock beds has not changed much since the 1820s. Collectors still work by hand with hammers, chisels, trowels, dental picks, and sieves. Gideon Mantell used these when he chiseled out *Iguanodon* bones embedded in one large rock called the "Mantle piece."

Fossil hunters also use hand lenses and microscopes. Sometimes a protective layer is built up with glue, varnish, or another finish. For larger samples, a plaster cast often supports the fossil. Most fossils are packed using a technology found in any kitchen—a sealable plastic bag.

1909
Burgess Shale Shows Soft Bodies

In the Burgess Pass of the Canadian Rocky Mountains, Charles Walcott finds fossils preserved in shale, a soft rock that preserves lacelike details such as the soft tissues of the Marella. The glimpse of life 505 million years ago is the earliest yet seen.

1944
New Dawn for the Dawn Redwood

Beside a small temple, a Chinese scientist discovers the dawn redwood, or metasequoia, growing. Common in fossil specimens 100 million years old, the tree had not been seen alive in recorded history. The 1944 find starts a search, and in 1948, scientists find a small wild grove in China as well.

1938
African Fisherman Hauls in History

A South African fisherman pulls up a five-foot fish he has never seen. He calls the local museum, whose curator, a naturalist, has also never seen the species. To her surprise, biologists identify it as a coelacanth, a prehistoric fish thought to be extinct for more than 50 million years.

| 1900 | 1910 | 1920 | 1930 | 1940 |

APPLICATION
Protecting Fossils and Dig Sites

The United States Antiquities Act of 1906 preserves and protects historic and prehistoric sites. The act requires collectors to have a permit to dig for or to pick up fossils on public lands such as national parks. It also requires that any major find be publicly and permanently preserved in a museum.

The United Nations also now designates World Heritage sites. For example, the original Burgess Shale find in Yoho National Park in Canada is now protected by international law. Since 1906, many states and provinces in Canada have enacted their own laws about land rights and the excavation and transport of fossils.

1974

"Lucy" and Upright Kin Found

Digging in Ethiopia, Donald Johanson finds an almost complete hominid skeleton. He names the fossil "Lucy," after a Beatles song. Lucy is over 3 million years old, is three and one-half feet tall, and has an upright stance or posture. A year later, Johanson's crew finds "The First Family," a group of 13 skeletons of the same species as Lucy.

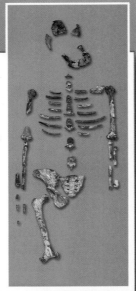

1990

Largest Tyrannosaurus, *"Sue"*

Out on a walk with her dog in the South Dakota badlands, amateur fossil hunter Sue Hendrickson discovers three huge bones jutting out of a cliff. Hendrickson finds the largest and most complete *T. rex* skeleton yet. The 67-million-year-old "Sue" is now on display in the Field Museum in Chicago, Illinois.

1953

Piltdown Man No Neanderthal

Scientists once applauded the discovery in 1912 of a "Neanderthal skull" in the Piltdown gravel pit, but a few had their doubts. In 1953, radioactive potassium dating proves the Piltdown man to be nothing more than the jaw of an orangutan placed beside human skull fragments.

1950   1960   1970   1980   1990

TECHNOLOGY

How Old Is a Fossil?

Before 1947, scientists used a method of fossil dating called relative dating. They assigned a date to a fossil according to the rock layer in which it was found. The deeper, or older, the layer, the older the fossil.

The discovery of radiometric dating in 1947 marked the first time a fossil's date could be pinpointed. Organic matter decays at a constant rate. So, by measuring the rate of decay, you can tell the age of the matter. Radiocarbon 14 is used to tell the age of a fossil that is less than 10,000 years old. Since most fossils are older than that, scientists use other methods.

Potassium-argon decays more slowly than carbon. It is a more common method of dating. All types of fossil dating have margins of error, or limits to accuracy.

1993

Oldest Fossils Are Too Small to See

Fossils discovered up to this point date back about 550 million years, to the dawn of the Cambrian Period. J. William Schopf identifies fossils of microorganisms scientifically dated to 3.4 billion years ago. This startling find near Australia's Marble Bar opens up a vast period of time and once again reshapes theories about life's beginnings.

RESOURCE CENTER
CLASSZONE.COM
Discover more about the latest fossil and living-fossil finds.

2000

TECHNOLOGY

Fossil Classification and DNA

There are many ways to classify fossils. Scientists look at bone structure, body posture, evidence of behavior, and environment. Microscopes are used to identify organisms too small for the eye to see. Study of DNA molecules helps to identify species when soft tissues remain intact, such as in fossils formed in amber or crystallized tree sap. In 1985, polymerase chain reaction (PCR) became the simplest method to study the DNA extracted from fossils. In PCR, parts of DNA can be copied billions of times in a few hours.

INTO THE FUTURE

Technology is sure to play a role in future fossil finds. Scientists can communicate via laptop computers and satellites, which allow the public to follow excavations as they occur.

Computer modeling helps scientists determine what incomplete skeletons looked like. It also helps them determine how dinosaurs and other living things once moved. Fossil finds can be combined with digitized information about modern living organisms and about environmental conditions. The model can test hypotheses or even help to formulate them.

Another area of technology that may become increasingly applied to fossils is DNA testing to identify and help date fossils. This is more complicated in fossilized bone, as the genetic material can be fragmented. But with time, scientists may discover new techniques to extract better genetic information. DNA is also the basis for cloning, which as yet can only be applied to living organisms. Perhaps in the future it can be applied to preserved remains.

ACTIVITIES

Writing About Science: Film Script

Write your own version of the story of life on Earth. Include drawings, photographs, or video clips to illustrate your story.

Reliving History

Think about the equipment archaeologists and paleontologists use on excavations. Think about their goals. Write a proposal to a local university or museum asking them to fund your excavation.

3 Population Dynamics

the BIG idea

Populations are shaped by interactions between organisms and the environment.

Key Concepts

SECTION

3.1 Populations have many characteristics.
Learn about the stages and factors that all populations have in common.

SECTION

3.2 Populations respond to pressures.
Learn how change can affect populations.

SECTION

3.3 Human populations have unique responses to change.
Learn how the responses of human populations are different from responses of other populations.

Internet Preview

CLASSZONE.COM

Chapter 3 online resources: Content Review, Visualization, three Resource Centers, Math Tutorial, Test Practice

This image was created by combining satellite shots of parts of Earth. What does it suggest about Earth's populations?

How Does Population Grow?

For every three human births there is one death. Use a bucket and water to represent the human population. For every 3 cups of water you add to the bucket, take away one cup.

Observe and Think
How did the water level rise—quickly, slowly, or steadily?

How Do Populations Differ?

Put about 40 marbles in a bowl. Remove any 10 marbles from the bowl and put them in another dish. Each dish of marbles represents a population.

Observe and Think
How would a chance event such as a fire affect these two populations differently?

Internet Activity: Population Dynamics

Go to **ClassZone.com** to learn more about the factors that describe a population. Find out how change in each of the factors can affect the population.

Observe and Think
How would a change in one factor affect the dynamics of a population?

NSTA
scilinks.org **SCiLINKS**

Limiting Factors **Code: MDL038**

Getting Ready to Learn

◀ CONCEPT REVIEW

- Living things change over time.
- Species adapt to their environment or become extinct.

◀ VOCABULARY REVIEW

See Glossary for definition.

species

CONTENT REVIEW
CLASSZONE.COM

Review concepts and vocabulary.

▶ TAKING NOTES

CHOOSE YOUR OWN STRATEGY

Take notes using one or more strategies from earlier chapters—**main idea and details** or **supporting main ideas.** You can also use other note-taking strategies that you might already know.

VOCABULARY STRATEGY

Think about a vocabulary term as a **magnet word** diagram. Write the other terms or ideas related to that term around it.

See the Note-Taking Handbook on pages R45–R51.

SCIENCE NOTEBOOK

Main Idea and Details

Supporting Main Ideas

species   POPULATION   size

age

spacing

3.1

Populations have many characteristics.

◀ BEFORE, you learned

- Species change over time
- Evolution is a process of change
- A habitat is an area that provides organisms with resources

▶ NOW, you will learn

- About stages in population dynamics
- About variables that define a population
- About changes that affect populations

VOCABULARY

population dynamics p. 81

carrying capacity p. 82

population size p. 84

population density p. 85

THINK ABOUT

How fast can a population grow?

How big can a population grow? Suppose you started with a pair of fruit flies. That single pair can produce 200 eggs. In three weeks, each pair from that batch could produce 200 flies of its own—producing up to 20,000 flies. Assume all eggs hatch—an event highly unlikely in the real world. After three weeks, 2 million fruit flies would be buzzing around the area. After just 17 generations, given ideal conditions (for the fruit fly, that is), the mass of fruit flies would exceed the mass of planet Earth.

CHOOSE YOUR OWN STRATEGY

Begin taking notes on the three stages of populations. Use a strategy from an earlier chapter or one that you already know.

Populations go through three stages.

Look closely at the fruit flies above. As a group of the same species living together in a particular area, they represent a population. The particular area in which a scientist studies a population may be as large as a mountain range or as small as a puddle. Scientists study how populations of organisms change as they interact with each other and the environment. Over time, the number of individuals in a population changes by increasing or decreasing. **Population dynamics** is the study of why populations change and what causes them to change. In this chapter you will learn about some of the important observations scientists have made about populations.

READING What is population dynamics?

One species of iguana may have several populations living on different islands. As a result, these iguana populations don't interact with each other. Yet there may be other populations of iguanas living on the islands made up of a different species.

Growth, Stability, and Decline

READING **TiP**

As you read about growth, stability, and decline, refer to the explanations on the graph.

As different as populations may be—whether cacti, finches, dragonflies, or iguanas—all populations go through the same three stages of change: growth, stability, and decline.

All living things need resources such as water, energy, and living space. Populations get their resources from the environment. However, the area a population occupies can support only so many individuals. **Carrying capacity** is the maximum number of individuals an ecosystem can support.

When a habitat contains enough resources to meet the needs of a population, the population grows rapidly. This growth stage of a population tends to be brief. On a graph, it looks like a sharp rise. The growth stage is followed by a period of stability, when the size of a population remains constant. For most populations, the stability stage is the longest stage of a population's existence. The stability stage is often followed by a decline in population size.

Population Change

The graph shows three stages of population change.

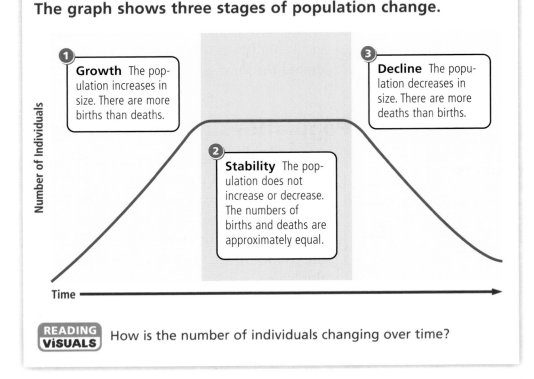

1 Growth The population increases in size. There are more births than deaths.

2 Stability The population does not increase or decrease. The numbers of births and deaths are approximately equal.

3 Decline The population decreases in size. There are more deaths than births.

Number of Individuals

Time

READING **VISUALS** How is the number of individuals changing over time?

During the growth stage, populations can increase according to two general patterns. One pattern is rapid growth, which increases at a greater and greater rate. Another pattern is gradual growth, which increases at a fairly steady rate. The two graphs below show the two different types of growth.

Population Growth

The graphs show two patterns of population growth.

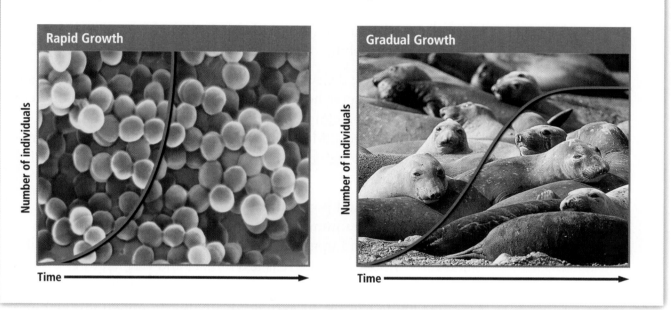

Darwin's Observations of Population Growth

In Chapter 1 you read about the observations and conclusions made by the naturalist Charles Darwin. In his book *On the Origin of Species* Darwin included important observations about population growth.

REMINDER

A species that is no longer living is considered extinct.

- All populations are able to grow rapidly.
- Populations tend to remain constant in size.
- There are limits to natural resources.
- Within a given population there is genetic variation.

Darwin recognized that organisms in most species have the ability to produce more than two surviving offspring. He knew that if there were no limits to growth, then populations would grow rapidly. However, Darwin also observed that in the real world there are natural limits to growth, so populations tend to stabilize. In order for a species to continue, individuals must be replaced as they die. This means that, on average, one member of a population must produce one surviving offspring. If the birth rate doesn't match the death rate, a population can decline until it becomes extinct.

Four characteristics define a population.

When scientists think about population dynamics, they consider four major characteristics. These characteristics include population size, population density, population spacing, and age structure.

Population Size

Population size is the number of individuals in a population at a given time. Even when the population size appears to be stable over time, changes can occur from year to year or from place to place. Population size varies from one habitat to another. It also varies within a single habitat.

An area where the summers are hot and the winters are cold is a good place to observe how population size might change at different times of year. For example, the population sizes of many insects change within a year. Mosquitoes that are all around you on warm summer evenings are nowhere in sight when the temperatures fall below freezing.

The size of plant populations can also change during the year. In the spring and summer you can see flowering plants across the deserts, woods, and mountains of North America. However, by fall and early winter, when there is less rainfall and temperatures drop, many of these plants die. Below is a picture of a southwestern desert in full bloom. During the springtime months of March through May, many deserts in the United States experience a change. There is a period of rapid growth as a variety of wildflowers begins to bloom.

When there is little rainfall a desert seems empty. After a rain, there is a brief time when plants bloom.

The availability of resources, such as water, increases plant growth. By summer the change in season brings higher temperatures and less rainfall. As a result, desert wildflowers experience a rapid decline in their population size.

CHECK YOUR READING What are two factors that affect population size?

Population Density

Population density is a measure of the number of individuals in a certain space at a particular time. Population density is related to population size. If a population's size increases and all of the individuals remain in the same area, then population density increases, too. There are more individuals living in the same amount of space. If the size of a population in a particular area decreases, density also decreases. Some species, such as bumblebees or mice, live in populations with high densities. Other species, such as blue herons or wolves, live in populations with low densities.

CHECK YOUR READING What is the difference between low density and high density?

Population Density

Density can change over time and over the entire area of the population.

Low Density

Herons are usually found alone or in pairs in marshy areas. Herons are an example of a low-density population.

High Density

Bees in a beehive are an example of a high-density population—many individuals are packed into a small area.

READING VISUALS COMPARE How does the number of herons in an area compare with the number of bees?

The distribution of a population across a large geographic area is its range. Within that range, population density may vary. For example, there may be more grasshoppers in the middle of a prairie than there are at the edges. The population density tends to be higher where more resources are available. Habitats located in the middle of a population range tend to have a greater population density than habitats located at the edges.

 CHECK YOUR READING How might population density vary within a range?

Population Spacing

Take a look around you as you walk through a local park. You might notice many flowers growing in open, sunny spots but few beneath the shade of large trees. The pattern in which the flowers grow is an example of population spacing. Scientists have observed three distinct patterns of spacing: clumped, uniform, and random.

In clumped spacing, individuals form small groups within a habitat. Animals like elephants clump because of their social nature. Clumping can also result from the way resources are distributed throughout a habitat. Salamanders that prefer moist, rotten logs may be clumped where logs have fallen in their habitat.

Population Spacing

Population spacing describes how individuals arrange themselves within a population.

Clumped

Individuals that clump themselves often gather around resources.

Uniform

Individuals that are uniformly arranged often compete for resources.

Random

Random patterns are rare and occur without regard to other individuals.

READING VISUALS Compare and contrast the way populations are spaced.

Some individuals live at a distance from each other. These individuals are uniformly spaced. Many plants that grow too close together become evenly spaced as individuals die out. Uniform spacing can protect saguaro cacti from competing for important resources in the desert. Individuals that aren't uniform or clumped space themselves randomly. Dandelions, for instance, grow no matter where other dandelions are growing.

Age Structure

Scientists divide a population into three groups based on age.

- postreproductive: organisms can no longer reproduce
- reproductive: organisms capable of reproduction
- prereproductive: organisms not yet able to reproduce

The age structure of a population affects how much it can grow. On the graph below, the postreproductive age range for humans is over 45, reproductive is 14 to 44 years of age, and prereproductive is 0 to 14.

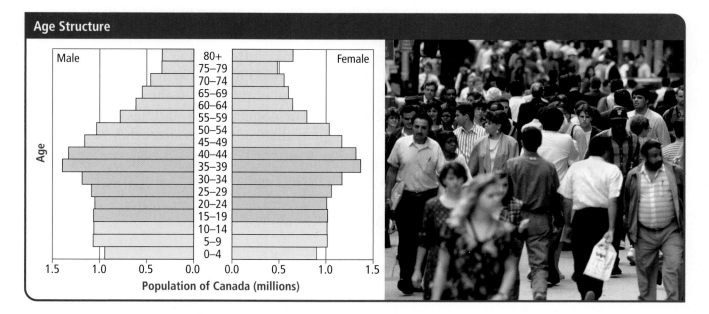

Age Structure

Male / Female

Age

80+
75–79
70–74
65–69
60–64
55–59
50–54
45–49
40–44
35–39
30–34
25–29
20–24
15–19
10–14
5–9
0–4

1.5   1.0   0.5   0.0   0.0   0.5   1.0   1.5

Population of Canada (millions)

Scientists can predict population change.

Scientists use these four factors—size, density, spacing, and age structure—to describe a population and to predict how it might change over time. Sometimes a population changes when a particular factor changes.

A population can change in response to its surroundings. Suppose a population of frogs is living in a pond where the water becomes saltier. Only those frogs that can survive in an environment with more salt will survive. Thus the population size of frogs will probably decrease as a result of the changing conditions. By looking at population size, scientists can predict how changes affect the population.

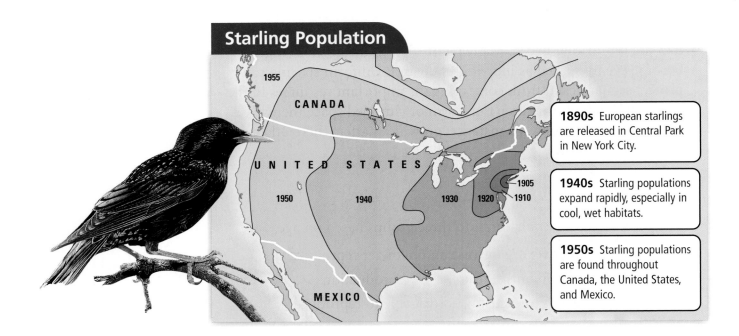

Starling Population

1955

CANADA

UNITED STATES

1950   1940   1930   1920   1905   1910

MEXICO

1890s European starlings are released in Central Park in New York City.

1940s Starling populations expand rapidly, especially in cool, wet habitats.

1950s Starling populations are found throughout Canada, the United States, and Mexico.

Scientists can also predict change by looking at the distribution of population. The story of the European starling provides a dramatic example of how the movement of organisms into or out of an area affects a population.

In 1890, the first starlings were introduced to the United States in New York City's Central Park. Their numbers went from 60 individuals to about 200 million in just over 100 years as they expanded on the North American continent. The population of starlings rose as starlings moved into new habitats that had the resources they needed.

Today large populations of starlings can still be found across the North American continent. Even within a given habitat, the population can vary. In Central Park, for example, you can find starlings in clumps, uniformly spaced, or randomly spaced.

VISUALIZATION
CLASSZONE.COM

Watch how a change in the environment can affect a population.

3.1 Review

KEY CONCEPTS

1. Describe the three stages of population growth.

2. Make a chart showing the four factors that affect population dynamics and an example of each.

3. Give an example of how a shift in age distribution can affect population growth.

CRITICAL THINKING

4. **Apply** Choose a population in your neighborhood. Describe its population spacing. Is it clumped, uniformly spaced, or randomly spaced?

5. **Compare/Contrast** How is population size related to population density? Your answer should mention area.

◯ CHALLENGE

6. **Predict** Explain how a heavy thunderstorm might affect the population density of birds living in the area.

MATH in SCIENCE

MATH TUTORIAL
CLASSZONE.COM
Click on Math Tutorial for more help finding the mean.

Making Sense of Samples

In a pond study, a biologist takes samples of water from four locations in one pond every three months. Using a microscope, she examines the samples and calculates the protist population for each location. The data table shows the number of protists found per milliliter in each sample of pond water.

Data Table: Number of protists per milliliter (mL) of pond water				
Location	**Fall**	**Winter**	**Spring**	**Summer**
Under the pier	150	50	120	410
Among the water lilies	200	80	180	500
Shallow area	220	90	200	360
Deepest area	80	60	100	390
Seasonal Average				

Example

Suppose you want to find the average number of protists per milliliter of pond water for that fall.

Step 1. Find the sum of all the data given above for "Fall."

Step 2. Divide this total by the number of data entries for "Fall."

Step 3. Round to nearest whole number.

$$150$$
$$200$$
$$220$$
$$+\ 80$$
$$650$$

$$650 \div 4 = 162.5$$

$$162.5 \rightarrow 163$$

ANSWER 163 protists per mL of pond water

For each season or location give the average number of protists.

1. Winter

2. Spring

3. Summer

4. Under the pier

5. Among the water lilies

6. Shallow area

7. Deepest area

8. Whole pond, yearlong

CHALLENGE Suppose the biologist only took samples from three areas in the pond. Which missing area would throw off the averages the most?

3.2 Populations respond to pressures.

◀ BEFORE, you learned

- Four characteristics are used to describe a population
- Scientists study these four characteristics to predict population change

▶ NOW, you will learn

- About limits to population growth
- How population density affects limiting factors
- About two reproductive strategies found within populations

VOCABULARY

immigration p. 91
emigration p. 91
limiting factor p. 92
opportunist p. 95
competitor p. 96

EXPLORE Population Density

How does population density vary?

PROCEDURE

1. Choose three different locations in your school where you can observe how many people enter and leave an area during a specific time period.

2. Position three people at each location a counter, a timekeeper, and a recorder.

3. Count the number of people who pass through the area for at least 2 minutes. Record the number.

4. Compare your data with the data collected by other groups.

WHAT DO YOU THINK?

- Where was the number of people the highest? the lowest?
- Explain what may have affected population density at each location.

MATERIALS

- stopwatch
- notebook

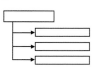

CHOOSE YOUR OWN STRATEGY
Use a strategy from an earlier chapter or one of your own to take notes on the main idea: *Population growth is limited.*

Population growth is limited.

No population can grow forever. Every population has a limit to its growth. For example, the cockroach has been around for more than 300 million years. This insect has outlived the dinosaurs and may persist long after humans have become extinct. Yet even if cockroaches became the only species on the planet, several factors would limit their population size.

Birth, Death, Immigration, and Emigration

When scientists study how a population changes, they must consider four things: birth, death, immigration, and emigration. There is even a simple formula to help scientists track population change.

Population change = (birth + immigration) − (death + emigration)

It is too simple to say that a high birth rate means population growth, or that many deaths mean population decline. **Immigration** is the movement of individuals into a population. For example, if a strong wind blows the seeds of a plant from one area into another, the new plant would be said to immigrate into the new area. Immigration can increase a population or help stabilize a declining population. Birth and immigration introduce individuals into a population.

Emigration is the movement of individuals out of a population. If resources become scarce within a habitat, some of the individuals might move to areas with greater supplies. Others may even die. Death and emigration remove individuals from a population.

CHECK YOUR READING List two factors that lead to population growth and two that lead to population decline.

Consider, for example, a flock of seagulls that flies inland during a storm. They stop at a city dump, where food is plentiful. These incoming seagulls become part of the seagull population that is already living at the dump. A raccoon population living in the same area has been eating the seagulls' eggs, causing the number of seagull births to decrease. If enough seagulls immigrate to the dump, the seagull population would increase, making up for the decrease in births. Immigration would help keep the population stable. The seagull population would also increase if part of the raccoon population moved away.

Limiting Factors

When a population is growing at a rapid rate, the birth rate is much higher than the death rate. That means that more individuals are being born than are dying during a particular time period. There are plenty of resources available, and the population size is increasing rapidly. Eventually, however, the population will stop growing, because a habitat can support only a limited number of organisms.

A **limiting factor** is a factor that prevents the continuing growth of a population in an ecosystem. Abiotic, or nonliving, limiting factors include air, light, and water. Other limiting factors can be living things, such as other organisms in the same population or individuals belonging to different species within the same area.

 CHECK YOUR READING What are two limiting factors?

Competition can occur between different populations sharing the same habitat. Competition can also occur among individuals of the same population. Suppose, for example, that a population of deer in a forest preserve were to increase, either through births or immigration. Population density at the forest preserve would go up. More and more deer in that area would be competing for the same amount of food.

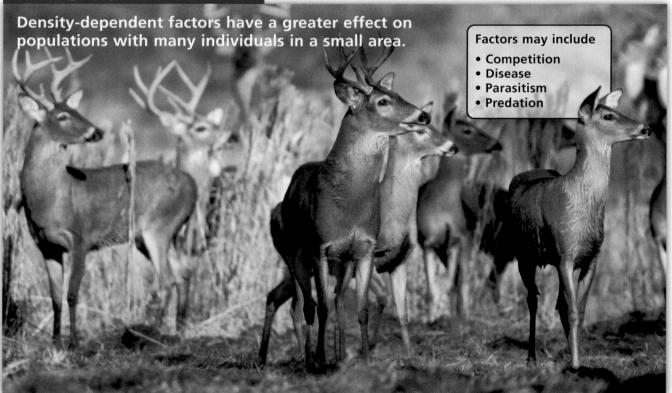

Density-Dependent Factors

Density-dependent factors have a greater effect on populations with many individuals in a small area.

Factors may include
- Competition
- Disease
- Parasitism
- Predation

Effects of Population Density

In the situation described above, the seagull population could decrease as a result of competition for food. Competition is an example of a density-dependent factor—that is, a limiting factor that affects a population when density is high. Disease is another density-dependent factor. The more crowded an area becomes, the easier it is for disease to spread, so more individuals are affected. If population density is low, there is less contact between individuals, which means that disease will spread more slowly. Density-dependent factors have a greater effect on the population as it grows. They can bring a population under control, because they apply more pressure to a growing population.

There are also density-independent factors. These limiting factors have the same effect on a population, whether it has a high density or a low density. Freezing temperatures could be considered a density-independent factor. A freeze might kill all of the flowering plants in an area, whether or not the population density is high. A natural event such as a wildfire is another example of a density-independent factor. When a wildfire occurs in a forest, it can wipe out an entire ecosystem.

CHECK YOUR READING How are limiting factors that are density-dependent different from limiting factors that are density-independent?

Density-Independent Factors

Density-independent factors are typically changes in weather. These factors affect low-density and high-density populations equally.

Factors may include
- Drought
- Hurricanes
- Tornados
- Fires
- Floods

Limiting factors include nonliving factors in the environment and natural events such as earthquakes, fires, and storms. During times of drought, there may not be enough food to meet the needs of all the organisms in an area. The quality of the food declines as well. For example, a lack of water may cause a population of trees to produce fewer pieces of fruit, and the fruit itself may be smaller. If there is little food available, a condition called famine arises. If the famine is severe, and if death rates exceed birth rates, then the population size will fall dramatically.

 How do limiting factors affect populations? Remember: a summary includes only the most important information.

Limiting factors affect human populations as well. However, humans have found different ways to help overcome many of these limits. In Section 3.3 you will read about how the human response to limits differs from that of other biological populations.

INVESTIGATE Limiting Factors

What limiting factors determine plant growth?

DESIGN —YOUR OWN— EXPERIMENT

Using the materials below, design an experiment to test how limiting factors such as sunlight or water can determine how well a plant population will grow.

PROCEDURE

1. Decide how to use the beans, soil, and water.
2. Write up your experimental procedure. Include any safety tips.

WHAT DO YOU THINK?

- What variables did you use in your experiment?
- What evidence do you expect to see to support the goal of your experiment?

CHALLENGE Conduct your experiment. Be sure to observe your beans daily and note which ones are most healthy. Make a chart and record your observations. The beans should grow for at least two weeks before you make your conclusion.

SKILL FOCUS
Designing experiments

MATERIALS
- 6 paper cups
- potting soil
- beans
- water

TIME
20 minutes

Populations have distinct reproductive survival strategies.

Although reproduction of offspring is not necessary for the survival of an individual organism, it is necessary for the survival of a species. Scientists studying populations observe patterns in the reproductive strategies used among species. There are two main strategies that many species use. There are also many species whose strategies fit somewhere in between.

Strategies of Opportunists

Opportunists are species that reproduce rapidly if their population falls below carrying capacity. They share many characteristics, including a short life span and the ability to reproduce large quantities of offspring. Their population size tends to change often, and opportunists live across many areas. Opportunists include algae, dandelions, bacteria, and insects. These species can reproduce and move across an area quickly. In addition, they can adapt quickly to environmental changes. Populations of opportunists often grow rapidly.

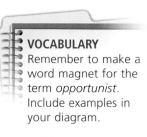

VOCABULARY
Remember to make a word magnet for the term *opportunist*. Include examples in your diagram.

Opportunists

Pine trees are opportunists that can spread across an area quickly.

Pine cones release huge amounts of pollen into the air.

Competitors

Wolves are examples of competitor species. These cubs will be cared for by adults until they are able to hunt.

Strategies of Competitors

You might be familiar with the term *competitor* as meaning an organism that struggles with another to get resources. Scientists who study population growth use the term *competitor* in another way. **Competitors** are species with adaptations that allow them to remain at or near their carrying capacity for long periods of time. Competitors have many characteristics that differ from those of opportunists.

Species that have a competitive reproductive strategy often live longer and have fewer offspring. Elephants and saguaro cacti are two examples of competitors. The offspring of competitors take longer to develop than those of opportunists. Also, animals with this strategy tend to take care of their young for a longer period of time. Competitors are not distributed across areas as widely as opportunists, but greater numbers of their offspring survive to reproductive age.

3.2 Review

KEY CONCEPTS	CRITICAL THINKING	⭕ CHALLENGE
1. What four factors do scientists consider when they measure population change?	**4. Analyze** Why would it be a mistake to predict population growth based on birth rate alone?	**6. Synthesize** There has been an oil spill along a waterway famous for its populations of seals, dolphins, and sea birds. Six months later, all populations show a decline. Explain what factors might have caused such a change and whether the oil spill was a density-dependent or density-independent factor or both.
2. Give two examples of density-dependent factors and two examples of density-independent factors.	**5. Apply** Give an example of a factor that limits a population near you.	
3. Other than life span, how do opportunists and competitors differ?		

Studying the Schools

There's a lot more to catching fish than putting a net or a line into the ocean. More and more these days, finding fish means looking at the big and changing picture of fish populations. Once you start fishing, you need to know when to stop fishing, as well as how to protect the other organisms in the ocean environment.

Density

If there are too few fish of a particular species in one area, it is best to leave them and look for a place with greater population density. By using the most suitable gear, the captain avoids killing or injuring fish and other animals that shouldn't be part of the catch.

Distribution

Some fish live alone, and some live in big groups, called schools. Some, called ground fish, stay on the bottom, while others swim near the surface. One way to see the distribution of fish is with sonar. An image made from sonar shows that a school of hake swims at a depth of about 320 meters (1050 ft).

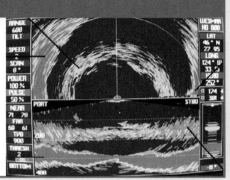

Partners in Research

Many boat captains set up partnerships with researchers to study fish and to help them to thrive. Sonar equipment is a tool shared by scientists and commercial fishers. Images are made by sending sound waves through the water and receiving the patterns of sound waves that bounce, or echo, back.

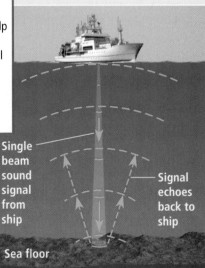

Single beam sound signal from ship

Signal echoes back to ship

Sea floor

EXPLORE

1. **INFER** Boat captains talk to each other about how many fish they catch and where and when they catch them. What are three reasons why this would be important?

2. **CHALLENGE** Suppose a fishing boat captain overfishes an organism that is a source of food for another organism. Describe what may happen to the other organism.

KEY CONCEPT

3.3 Human populations have unique responses to change.

◀ **BEFORE,** you learned

- Over time, all populations stop growing
- All populations are affected by limiting factors
- Reproductive strategies include opportunism and competition

▶ **NOW,** you will learn

- How human populations differ from other populations
- How humans adapt to the environment
- How human populations affect the environment

VOCABULARY

pollution p. 104

EXPLORE Population Change

How can you predict human population growth?

PROCEDURE

1. Copy the graph on the right. The graph shows populaton growth expected in the United States with an increase in both birth and death rates and with steady immigration.

2. The graph shows a medium rate of growth. Draw another line to show what low population growth might look like. Label it.

3. Explain the patterns of birth rates, death rates, and immigration that might be likely to result in low population growth.

WHAT DO YOU THINK?

- How would the projected U.S. population size change if there were no immigration?
- How might an increase in immigration affect expected birth rates?

MATERIALS
- graph paper
- colored pencils

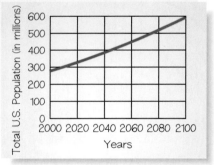

Human populations differ from populations of other species.

CHOOSE YOUR OWN STRATEGY
Begin taking notes on the differences between human populations and populations of other species.

Humans are not the fastest or the largest organisms on Earth. They must get food from other organisms. Humans have a limited sense of smell, and the vision of a human is inferior to that of a hawk. However, the human population now dominates our planet. Why? Humans are able to shape their environment. Humans are also able to determine their own biological reproduction. Because humans can control many factors that limit growth, Earth's carrying capacity for humans has increased. Two key factors that have increased Earth's carrying capacity for humans are habitat expansion and technology.

Habitat Expansion

Individuals who study the history of ancient peoples know that populations of humans have spread throughout the world. Discoveries of ancient human tools and skeletons indicate that the first human populations lived on the continent now known as Africa. Over time, human populations have spread over nearly the entire planet.

The word *habitat* refers to a place where an organism can live. Humans have expanded their habitats, and thus the population has grown. Humans can survive in many different environments by adding air conditioning or heat to regulate indoor temperature. They can design and build shelters that protect them from harsh environments.

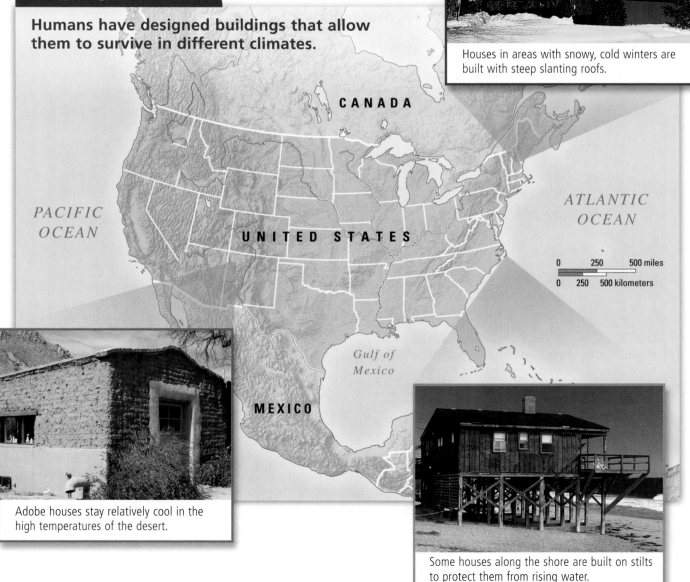

Adapting to Climate

Humans have designed buildings that allow them to survive in different climates.

CANADA

PACIFIC OCEAN

UNITED STATES

ATLANTIC OCEAN

0   250   500 miles
0   250   500 kilometers

Gulf of Mexico

MEXICO

Houses in areas with snowy, cold winters are built with steep slanting roofs.

Adobe houses stay relatively cool in the high temperatures of the desert.

Some houses along the shore are built on stilts to protect them from rising water.

Technology

Limited resources and environmental conditions such as climate do not affect human population growth the way they do the growth of other biological populations. Humans have found ways to fit themselves into almost every climate by altering their clothing, shelter, diet, and means of transportation.

Scientific discoveries and the advances of technology—such as improved sanitation and medical care—have increased the standard of living and the life expectancy of many humans. Important goods such as food and shelter are manufactured and shipped around the world. Water, which is a limited resource, can be transported through pipes and dams to irrigate fields or reach normally dry areas. Water can also be purified for drinking or treated before it is released back into the environment.

CHECK YOUR READING How does technology help humans get resources they need for survival?

Technology

Transporting Water

Food is often grown on large farms. Humans have developed irrigation systems to carry water to the fields.

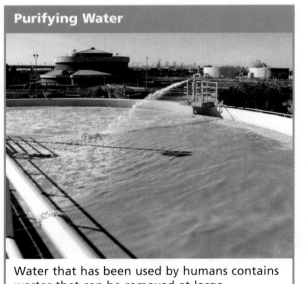

Purifying Water

Water that has been used by humans contains wastes that can be removed at large watertreatment plants.

Human populations are growing.

As you've read, humans have developed solutions to many limits on growth. These solutions have allowed the human population to grow rapidly. Scientists are studying the history of this growth and trying to predict whether it will continue or change.

History of Human Population Growth

RESOURCE CENTER
CLASSZONE.COM

Learn more about world-wide human population growth.

Until about 300 years ago, the human population grew slowly. Disease, climate, and the availability of resources limited population size. Most offspring did not survive to adulthood. Even though birthrates were high, death rates were also high.

Notice the human population on the graph below. Many historical events have affected its growth. For example, the development of agriculture provided humans with a more stable food source. This in turn helped support human population growth. Today, populations across many parts of the world are increasing rapidly. Scientists identify three conditions that allow for rapid growth: the availability of resources, lack of predators, and survival of offspring to reproductive age. As these conditions change, so does the population.

Population Projections

To help prepare for the future, scientists make predictions called population projections. Population projections forecast how a population will change, based on its present size and age structure. Population projections provide a picture of what the future might look like. Using population projections, government agencies, resource managers, and economists can plan to meet the future needs of a population.

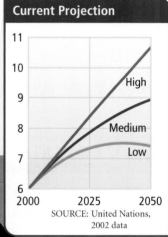

Current Projection

SOURCE: United Nations, 2002 data

The blowout of the graph shows three projections for the human population size. Experts disagree about the rate at which the population will grow.

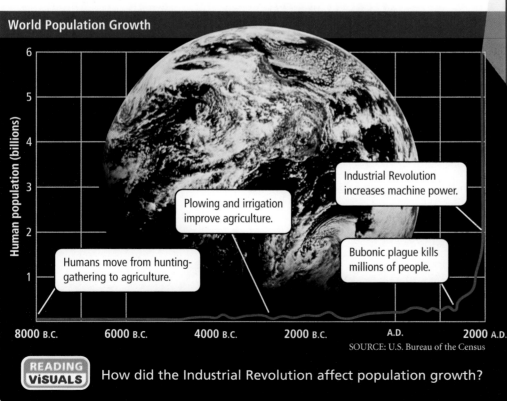

World Population Growth

Human population (billions)

Humans move from hunting-gathering to agriculture.

Plowing and irrigation improve agriculture.

Industrial Revolution increases machine power.

Bubonic plague kills millions of people.

8000 B.C.   6000 B.C.   4000 B.C.   2000 B.C.   A.D.   2000 A.D.

SOURCE: U.S. Bureau of the Census

READING VISUALS How did the Industrial Revolution affect population growth?

In addition to population size and age structure, scientists making population projections consider other factors. These factors include the ages of individuals having children. The average number of offspring produced by an individual also affects projections. In addition, life expectancy and health in a particular population affect population growth.

The factors affecting population growth vary from society to society. The human population in the African country Botswana provides an example of how disease and health can affect population growth.

In some African countries, death rates due to HIV/AIDS have lowered population projections for the year 2015 by almost 18 percent. Botswana's population will decline, because more than 30 percent of adults are infected with HIV/AIDS. So many people in Botswana have already died of HIV/AIDS that the average life expectancy has dropped from 63 years of age in the late 1980s to 32 years in 2003. Consider the impact this will have on the population's age structure. Because many people who die from HIV/AIDS are in their reproductive years, the long-term effects on population growth will be significant.

CHECK YOUR READING What factors do scientists consider when they make population projections?

INVESTIGATE Population

How can you graph population growth data for your area?

PROCEDURE

1. Use local population data taken from each census over five decades.

2. On graph paper, mark off five decades along the x–axis. Make a y–axis to show population size.

3. Plot the census information for each decade as a line graph.

WHAT DO YOU THINK?

- How did the local population change over time?
- What do you think accounted for the change?

CHALLENGE Based on the trend you see so far, how might the population change in the future? Use another color to extend the line on your graph to project population change over the next five decades. Explain why you think the population will change as you have predicted.

SKILL FOCUS
Graphing data

MATERIALS
- graph paper
- census data
- 2 colored pencils

TIME
30 minutes

Human population growth affects the environment.

You have read that extinction of species is a part of the history of life on Earth. The ways a population uses and disposes of resources have a great impact on local and global environments. As the human population continues to grow and use more resources, it contributes to the decline and extinction of other populations.

Some scientists estimate that over 99 percent of the species that have ever existed on Earth are now extinct. Most of these species vanished long before humans came on the scene. However, some experts are concerned that human activity is causing other species to become extinct at a much higher rate than they would naturally. Human populations put pressure on the environment in many ways, including

RESOURCE CENTER
CLASSZONE.COM

Find out more on introduced species in the United States.

- introduction of new species
- pollution
- overfishing

Introduction of New Species

Travelers have introduced new species to areas both on purpose and by accident. Many species introduced to an area provide benefits, such as food or beauty. Some species, however, cause harm to ecosystems. One example of an introduced species is the zebra mussel. An ocean vessel accidentally released zebra mussels from Europe into the Great Lakes region of the United States. With no natural predators that consume them, the mussels have reproduced quickly, invading all of the Great Lakes, the Mississippi River, and the Hudson River. The mussels compete with native species for food and affect water quality, endangering the ecosystem.

Kudzu is another introduced species. In the 1930s, kudzu was used in the southeastern United States to keep soil from being washed away. The plants, which have beautiful purple flowers, were imported from Japan. Starch made from kudzu is also a popular ingredient in some Asian recipes. However, populations of the kudzu vines planted in the United States have grown too far and too fast. Kudzu grows as much as 0.3 meters (about a foot) per day, killing trees and other plants living in the same area.

The kudzu plant, though at one time considered beautiful, is threatening other species.

Pollution

While human activities might cause some populations to decline, they can also cause other populations to grow. Sometimes this population growth causes pollution and habitat disturbance. **Pollution** is the addition of harmful substances to the environment. One example of such an activity is large-scale hog farming.

Human demands for pork combined with a growing human population have caused the hog farming industry to expand. Between 1987 and 2001, the hog population in North Carolina grew from 2.6 million to 10 million. These 10 million hogs produced more than 50,000 tons of waste each day. Wastes from large populations of hogs affect water supplies, soil, and air quality.

Pollution has also affected the Salton Sea in southeastern California. The growing demand for goods and agriculture has led to chemical dumping from industries and pesticide runoff from nearby farms. The rivers that run into the lake carry high levels of harmful chemicals such as DDT. Local birds that live and feed in this area have weakened shells that cannot support baby birds. Pollution has also caused fish to become deformed.

Large-scale hog farms affect water, soil, and air quality.

Pollution

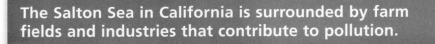

The Salton Sea in California is surrounded by farm fields and industries that contribute to pollution.

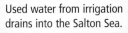

Used water from irrigation drains into the Salton Sea.

Overfishing

Fish and crustaceans such as shrimp and lobsters have long been an important food source for many people. In the 1900s, the techniques and equipment that fishers used allowed them to catch so many fish that fish populations began to decrease. As the human population has continued to grow, so has the demand for fish. However, if fish do not survive long enough in the wild, they do not have the chance to reproduce. Many species have been so overfished that their populations may not recover.

Lobster fishing in particular has supported coastal communities in the northeastern United States for generations. But the demand for this food source has caused populations to decline. Areas that fishers trapped for years may now have only a small population of lobsters. And the lobsters fishers are catching may not be as large as those from earlier decades.

In order to help lobster populations recover, laws have been enforced to protect their life cycle and reproduction. Today, people who trap lobsters are required to release females with eggs. They are also allowed to keep only mature lobsters. Younger lobsters are returned to the waters to mature and reproduce. Efforts like these help protect the lobster population and secure the jobs of fishers by helping fish populations remain stable.

Fishers harvesting lobster measure the tails of the animals they catch. A lobster that is too small is returned to the sea to allow it to grow.

CHECK YOUR READING Describe how overfishing would affect resources.

3.3 Review

KEY CONCEPTS

1. What factors—other than birth, death, immigration, and emigration—must scientists consider when making projections of human population?

2. Give an example of how Earth's carrying capacity for humans has increased.

3. What are three ways that humans affect other populations?

CRITICAL THINKING

4. **Infer** Consider the effect of HIV/AIDS on Botswana's human population. How might age structure affect Botswana's population growth?

5. **Analyze** Do you think it is possible to predict the maximum number of humans that Earth can support? Why or why not?

CHALLENGE

6. **Apply** Identify a challenge faced by the human population in your state. Explain how the challenge is related to pollution, introduction of new species, habitat disturbance, or overfishing.

CHAPTER INVESTIGATION

Sustainable Resource Management

OVERVIEW AND PURPOSE Wood is a renewable resource, but the demand for wood is continuing to grow worldwide. Humans are harvesting trees more quickly than trees have the ability to grow and replace themselves. The result is a forest in decline. In this activity you will

- model what happens when trees are harvested to meet the needs of a growing population
- calculate the rate at which the population of a renewable resource declines

▶ Question

How can people meet the ongoing human demand for wood without using all the trees? You will use the increasing human demand for wood to determine how overuse of a resource might affect a population. What would you like to discover about resource management? Write a question that begins with *Which, How, Why, When,* or *What.*

▶ Procedure

1. Copy the data table on page 107 into your **Science Notebook.**

2. In your group of classmates, decide who will fill each of the following roles: forest, timer, forest manager, harvester/record keeper.

3. **Forest:** Get a coffee can of 120 craft sticks. These sticks represent the available tree supply.

4. **Timer:** Sound off each 15-second interval and each minute.

MATERIALS
- coffee can with 120 craft sticks
- bundle of 32 craft sticks
- stopwatch

5 **Forest Manager:** Get 32 sticks from the teacher. You will add 1 new tree every 15 seconds by putting a stick in the coffee can.

6 **Harvester:** At the end of the first minute, cut down 1 tree by removing 1 stick from the coffee can. At the end of the second minute, cut down 2 trees; at the end of the third, cut down 4 trees. At the end of each additional minute cut down twice as many trees as you did before. This represents the doubling of the demand for trees based on human population growth.

▶ Observe and Analyze

1. **CALCULATE** At the end of each minute, add 4 trees, but subtract twice as many trees as you subtracted the minute before.

2. **RECORD AND CALCULATE** Complete the chart. How many trees are left in the forest after 8 minutes of harvesting?

▶ Conclude

1. **INFER** What effect does increasing human population growth have on forests?

2. **EVALUATE** Was the forest always shrinking?

3. **EVALUATE** How does this investigation help you to answer or change your question about resource management?

4. **IDENTIFY LIMITS** What aspects of this investigation fail to model the natural habitat?

5. **APPLY** What other renewable resources need sustainable management?

▶ INVESTIGATE Further

CHALLENGE Explain how you could use the data gathered in this investigation to develop methods of sustainable resource management.

Sustainable Resource Management

Table 1. Rate of Harvest

Minutes	Number of Trees at Start of Minute	Number of New Trees	Number of Trees Harvested	Number of Trees at End of Minute
1	120	+4	−1	123
2				
3				
4				
5				
6				
7				
8				

Chapter Review

Populations are shaped by interactions between organisms and the environment.

CONTENT REVIEW
CLASSZONE.COM

KEY CONCEPTS SUMMARY

3.1 Populations have many characteristics.

- Populations go through three stages:
  growth
  stability
  decline
- Four characteristics define a population:
  size
  density
  spacing
  age structure
- Scientists can predict population changes.

VOCABULARY
population dynamics p. 81
carrying capacity p. 82
population size p. 84
population density p. 85

3.2 Populations respond to pressures.

Populations change as they respond to pressures from limiting factors.

Two types of limiting factors are density dependent and density independent.

VOCABULARY
immigration p. 91
emigration p. 91
limiting factor p. 92
opportunist p. 95
competitor p. 96

3.3 Human populations have unique responses to change.

Humans can control many factors that limit most biological populations.

VOCABULARY
pollution p. 104

Reviewing Vocabulary

Describe how the vocabulary terms in the following pairs are related to each other. Explain the relationship in a one- or two-sentence answer. Underline each vocabulary term in your answers.

1. population dynamics and carrying capacity

2. immigration and emigration

3. limiting factor and population density

4. opportunists and competitors

Reviewing Key Concepts

Multiple Choice *Choose the letter of the best answer.*

5. The study of changes in a population over time and the factors that affect these changes is called population
   - **a.** stability
   - **b.** dynamics
   - **c.** spacing
   - **d.** density

6. A population that has reached its maximum size in a given area is said to have reached its
   - **a.** population range
   - **b.** gradual growth
   - **c.** carrying capacity
   - **d.** population projection

7. Assuming there is no immigration or emigration, a population size will remain constant if
   - **a.** the birth rate equals the death rate
   - **b.** the birth rate exceeds the death rate
   - **c.** the death rate exceeds the birth rate
   - **d.** the birth rate increases constantly

8. Distinct patterns in a population such as clumped, uniform, or random populations are examples of population
   - **a.** density
   - **b.** spacing
   - **c.** growth
   - **d.** dynamics

9. Which factors affect the size and growth of a population?
   - **a.** number of births and deaths
   - **b.** emigration and immigration
   - **c.** competition between populations
   - **d.** all of the above

10. A limiting factor that depends on the size of the population in a given area is a
    - **a.** density-dependent factor
    - **b.** density-independent factor
    - **c.** reproduction survival strategy
    - **d.** carrying capacity

11. Density-independent limiting factors include
    - **a.** predators
    - **b.** parasites
    - **c.** floods
    - **d.** competition

12. Which are abiotic factors in an environment?
    - **a.** disease and parasites
    - **b.** air, light, and water
    - **c.** pollution and overfishing
    - **d.** competition and predators

13. Which is an example of competition for resources?
    - **a.** individuals in a population feeding on the same food sources
    - **b.** movement of seagulls into a population of other seagulls
    - **c.** an increase in the population of raccoons in a particular environment at a steady rate
    - **d.** a population of fruit trees producing less fruit because of drought

14. Two factors that have increased Earth's carrying capacity for humans are habitat expansion, and
    - **a.** habitat disturbance
    - **b.** strategies of competitors
    - **c.** strategies of opportunists
    - **d.** technology

Short Answer *Write a short answer to each question.*

15. What factors might affect the density of a population?

16. What is the age structure of a population?

17. Describe three factors that account for the rapid growth of the human population during the past 500 years.

Thinking Critically

18. ANALYZE Under what conditions does gradual growth in a population occur?

19. COMMUNICATE Describe four observations that Darwin made about population growth.

20. PREDICT The graph below shows the exponential growth rate of a colony of unicellular organisms. If the population continues to grow at the same rate during the next 2 hours, what will the population be after 10 hours? Explain your answer.

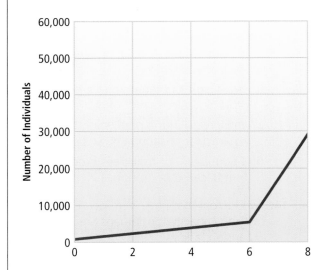

21. PREDICT In a certain population 35 percent of the individuals are under the age of 20. What predictions might you make about the size of the population in 10 years?

22. PROVIDE EXAMPLES What limiting factors might cause the carrying capacity of a population to change? Provide at least three examples. Describe how the population might change.

23. SYNTHESIZE What is an example of a density-independent factor that has affected a human population? Describe how this factor changed the population.

24. INFER Wolves are the natural predators of moose. Both populations are found on an island in the middle of Lake Superior. During one season, the population of moose increased dramatically. What could have caused the increase in the moose population?

25. EVALUATE Why do you suppose that the growth rate of human populations differs dramatically in different countries?

26. SYNTHESIZE Human activity has resulted in the decline of many populations of other species. Choose one example of how humans have put pressure on species around the world and describe ways that humans can avoid causing continued decreases in these populations.

the BIG idea

27. INFER Look again at the picture on pages 78–79. Now that you have finished the chapter, how would you change or add details to your answer to the question on the photograph?

28. SUMMARIZE Write one or more paragraphs describing the factors that affect population size, density, and age structure. Use the following terms in your descriptions.

immigration	density-dependent factors
emigration	density-independent factors
limiting factors	

UNIT PROJECTS

If you need to do an experiment for your unit project, gather the materials. Be sure to allow enough time to observe results before the project is due.

Analyzing Data

The graph below is an example of a population growth curve.

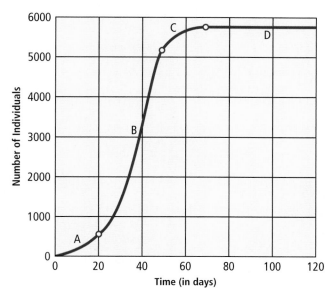

Use the graph to answer the questions below.

1. What does the time interval marked *D* represent?
  a. Population is decreasing.
  b. Carrying capacity has been reached.
  c. Birth rates exceed death rates.
  d. Population is growing.

2. Which time interval on the graph represents gradual growth?
  a. interval A and interval B
  b. interval C and interval D
  c. interval C only
  d. interval D only

3. During which time interval do limiting factors in a population begin to have an effect on the population growth?
  a. interval A only
  b. interval B only
  c. interval C only
  d. interval C and interval D

4. This graph represents a typical
  a. gradual curve
  b. rapid curve
  c. slow curve
  d. flat curve

5. What conclusion can you draw from the information in the graph?
  a. Density-dependent factors have had no effect on the population shown on the graph.
  b. The graph indicates an absence of disease and a supply of unlimited resources.
  c. Resources have become more available, so the population continues to increase exponentially.
  d. As resources become less available, the population rate slows or stops.

Extended Response

6. What part of the graph above shows the growth of the human population during the last 500 years? Explain. What are some factors that might allow the human population to reach its carrying capacity?

7. Choose a population of organisms in your area. Describe the limiting factors that may affect the growth of that population. Make sure you include both density-dependent and density-independent factors in your discussion.

Student Resource Handbooks

Scientific Thinking Handbook

Making Observations

An **observation** is an act of noting and recording an event, characteristic, behavior, or anything else detected with an instrument or with the senses.

Observations allow you to make informed hypotheses and to gather data for experiments. Careful observations often lead to ideas for new experiments. There are two categories of observations:

- **Quantitative observations** can be expressed in numbers and include records of time, temperature, mass, distance, and volume.

- **Qualitative observations** include descriptions of sights, sounds, smells, and textures.

EXAMPLE

A student dissolved 30 grams of Epsom salts in water, poured the solution into a dish, and let the dish sit out uncovered overnight. The next day, she made the following observations of the Epsom salt crystals that grew in the dish.

Table 1. Observations of Epsom Salt Crystals

Quantitative Observations	Qualitative Observations
• mass = 30 g • mean crystal length = 0.5 cm • longest crystal length = 2 cm	• Crystals are clear. • Crystals are long, thin, and rectangular. • White crust has formed around edge of dish.

> To determine the mass, the student found the mass of the dish before and after growing the crystals and then used subtraction to find the difference.

> The student measured several crystals and calculated the mean length. (To learn how to calculate the mean of a data set, see page R36.)

> Photographs or sketches are useful for recording qualitative observations.

Epsom salt crystals

MORE ABOUT OBSERVING

- Make quantitative observations whenever possible. That way, others will know exactly what you observed and be able to compare their results with yours.

- It is always a good idea to make qualitative observations too. You never know when you might observe something unexpected.

Predicting and Hypothesizing

A **prediction** is an expectation of what will be observed or what will happen. A **hypothesis** is a tentative explanation for an observation or scientific problem that can be tested by further investigation.

EXAMPLE

Suppose you have made two paper airplanes and you wonder why one of them tends to glide farther than the other one.

1. Start by asking a question.

2. Make an educated guess. After examination, you notice that the wings of the airplane that flies farther are slightly larger than the wings of the other airplane.

3. Write a prediction based upon your educated guess, in the form of an "If . . . , then . . ." statement. Write the independent variable after the word *if*, and the dependent variable after the word *then*.

4. To make a hypothesis, explain why you think what you predicted will occur. Write the explanation after the word *because*.

1. Why does one of the paper airplanes glide farther than the other?

2. The size of an airplane's wings may affect how far the airplane will glide.

3. Prediction: If I make a paper airplane with larger wings, then the airplane will glide farther.

> To read about independent and dependent variables, see page R30.

4. Hypothesis: If I make a paper airplane with larger wings, then the airplane will glide farther, because the additional surface area of the wing will produce more lift.

> Notice that the part of the hypothesis after *because* adds an explanation of why the airplane will glide farther.

MORE ABOUT HYPOTHESES

- The results of an experiment cannot prove that a hypothesis is correct. Rather, the results either support or do not support the hypothesis.

- Valuable information is gained even when your hypothesis is not supported by your results. For example, it would be an important discovery to find that wing size is not related to how far an airplane glides.

- In science, a hypothesis is supported only after many scientists have conducted many experiments and produced consistent results.

Inferring

An **inference** is a logical conclusion drawn from the available evidence and prior knowledge. Inferences are often made from observations.

EXAMPLE

A student observing a set of acorns noticed something unexpected about one of them. He noticed a white, soft-bodied insect eating its way out of the acorn.

The student recorded these observations.

Observations

- There is a hole in the acorn, about 0.5 cm in diameter, where the insect crawled out.
- There is a second hole, which is about the size of a pinhole, on the other side of the acorn.
- The inside of the acorn is hollow.

Here are some inferences that can be made on the basis of the observations.

Inferences

- The insect formed from the material inside the acorn, grew to its present size, and ate its way out of the acorn.
- The insect crawled through the smaller hole, ate the inside of the acorn, grew to its present size, and ate its way out of the acorn.
- An egg was laid in the acorn through the smaller hole. The egg hatched into a larva that ate the inside of the acorn, grew to its present size, and ate its way out of the acorn.

When you make inferences, be sure to look at all of the evidence available and combine it with what you already know.

MORE ABOUT INFERENCES

Inferences depend both on observations and on the knowledge of the people making the inferences. Ancient people who did not know that organisms are produced only by similar organisms might have made an inference like the first one. A student today might look at the same observations and make the second inference. A third student might have knowledge about this particular insect and know that it is never small enough to fit through the smaller hole, leading her to the third inference.

Identifying Cause and Effect

In a **cause-and-effect relationship,** one event or characteristic is the result of another. Usually an effect follows its cause in time.

There are many examples of cause-and-effect relationships in everyday life.

Cause	Effect
Turn off a light.	Room gets dark.
Drop a glass.	Glass breaks.
Blow a whistle.	Sound is heard.

Scientists must be careful not to infer a cause-and-effect relationship just because one event happens after another event. When one event occurs after another, you cannot infer a cause-and-effect relationship on the basis of that information alone. You also cannot conclude that one event caused another if there are alternative ways to explain the second event. A scientist must demonstrate through experimentation or continued observation that an event was truly caused by another event.

EXAMPLE

Make an Observation

Suppose you have a few plants growing outside. When the weather starts getting colder, you bring one of the plants indoors. You notice that the plant you brought indoors is growing faster than the others are growing. You cannot conclude from your observation that the change in temperature was the cause of the increased plant growth, because there are alternative explanations for the observation. Some possible explanations are given below.

- The humidity indoors caused the plant to grow faster.

- The level of sunlight indoors caused the plant to grow faster.

- The indoor plant's being noticed more often and watered more often than the outdoor plants caused it to grow faster.

- The plant that was brought indoors was healthier than the other plants to begin with.

To determine which of these factors, if any, caused the indoor plant to grow faster than the outdoor plants, you would need to design and conduct an experiment.

See pages R28–R35 for information about designing experiments.

Recognizing Bias

Television, newspapers, and the Internet are full of experts claiming to have scientific evidence to back up their claims. How do you know whether the claims are really backed up by good science?

Bias is a slanted point of view, or personal prejudice. The goal of scientists is to be as objective as possible and to base their findings on facts instead of opinions. However, bias often affects the conclusions of researchers, and it is important to learn to recognize bias.

When scientific results are reported, you should consider the source of the information as well as the information itself. It is important to critically analyze the information that you see and read.

SOURCES OF BIAS

There are several ways in which a report of scientific information may be biased. Here are some questions that you can ask yourself:

1. **Who is sponsoring the research?**

   Sometimes, the results of an investigation are biased because an organization paying for the research is looking for a specific answer. This type of bias can affect how data are gathered and interpreted.

2. **Is the research sample large enough?**

   Sometimes research does not include enough data. The larger the sample size, the more likely that the results are accurate, assuming a truly random sample.

3. **In a survey, who is answering the questions?**

   The results of a survey or poll can be biased. The people taking part in the survey may have been specifically chosen because of how they would answer. They may have the same ideas or lifestyles. A survey or poll should make use of a random sample of people.

4. **Are the people who take part in a survey biased?**

   People who take part in surveys sometimes try to answer the questions the way they think the researcher wants them to answer. Also, in surveys or polls that ask for personal information, people may be unwilling to answer questions truthfully.

SCIENTIFIC BIAS

It is also important to realize that scientists have their own biases because of the types of research they do and because of their scientific viewpoints. Two scientists may look at the same set of data and come to completely different conclusions because of these biases. However, such disagreements are not necessarily bad. In fact, a critical analysis of disagreements is often responsible for moving science forward.

Identifying Faulty Reasoning

Faulty reasoning is wrong or incorrect thinking. It leads to mistakes and to wrong conclusions. Scientists are careful not to draw unreasonable conclusions from experimental data. Without such caution, the results of scientific investigations may be misleading.

EXAMPLE

Scientists try to make generalizations based on their data to explain as much about nature as possible. If only a small sample of data is looked at, however, a conclusion may be faulty. Suppose a scientist has studied the effects of the El Niño and La Niña weather patterns on flood damage in California from 1989 to 1995. The scientist organized the data in the bar graph below.

The scientist drew the following conclusions:

1. The La Niña weather pattern has no effect on flooding in California.
2. When neither weather pattern occurs, there is almost no flood damage.
3. A weak or moderate El Niño produces a small or moderate amount of flooding.
4. A strong El Niño produces a lot of flooding.

Flood and Storm Damage in California

Estimated damage (millions of dollars) vs. *Starting year of season (July 1–June 30)*

- Weak–moderate El Niño
- Strong El Niño

SOURCE: *Governor's Office of Emergency Services, California*

For the six-year period of the scientist's investigation, these conclusions may seem to be reasonable. However, a six-year study of weather patterns may be too small of a sample for the conclusions to be supported. Consider the following graph, which shows information that was gathered from 1949 to 1997.

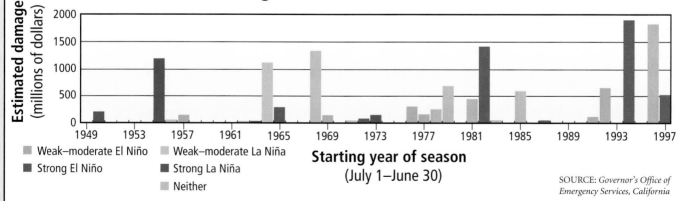

Flood and Storm Damage in California from 1949 to 1997

Estimated damage (millions of dollars) vs. *Starting year of season (July 1–June 30)*

- Weak–moderate El Niño
- Strong El Niño
- Weak–moderate La Niña
- Strong La Niña
- Neither

SOURCE: *Governor's Office of Emergency Services, California*

The only one of the conclusions that all of this information supports is number 3: a weak or moderate El Niño produces a small or moderate amount of flooding. By collecting more data, scientists can be more certain of their conclusions and can avoid faulty reasoning.

Analyzing Statements

To **analyze** a statement is to examine its parts carefully. Scientific findings are often reported through media such as television or the Internet. A report that is made public often focuses on only a small part of research. As a result, it is important to question the sources of information.

Evaluate Media Claims

To **evaluate** a statement is to judge it on the basis of criteria you've established. Sometimes evaluating means deciding whether a statement is true.

Reports of scientific research and findings in the media may be misleading or incomplete. When you are exposed to this information, you should ask yourself some questions so that you can make informed judgments about the information.

1. **Does the information come from a credible source?**

   Suppose you learn about a new product and it is stated that scientific evidence proves that the product works. A report from a respected news source may be more believable than an advertisement paid for by the product's manufacturer.

2. **How much evidence supports the claim?**

   Often, it may seem that there is new evidence every day of something in the world that either causes or cures an illness. However, information that is the result of several years of work by several different scientists is more credible than an advertisement that does not even cite the subjects of the experiment.

3. **How much information is being presented?**

   Science cannot solve all questions, and scientific experiments often have flaws. A report that discusses problems in a scientific study may be more believable than a report that addresses only positive experimental findings.

4. **Is scientific evidence being presented by a specific source?**

   Sometimes scientific findings are reported by people who are called experts or leaders in a scientific field. But if their names are not given or their scientific credentials are not reported, their statements may be less credible than those of recognized experts.

Differentiate Between Fact and Opinion

Sometimes information is presented as a fact when it may be an opinion. When scientific conclusions are reported, it is important to recognize whether they are based on solid evidence. Again, you may find it helpful to ask yourself some questions.

1. **What is the difference between a fact and an opinion?**

   A **fact** is a piece of information that can be strictly defined and proved true. An **opinion** is a statement that expresses a belief, value, or feeling. An opinion cannot be proved true or false. For example, a person's age is a fact, but if someone is asked how old they feel, it is impossible to prove the person's answer to be true or false.

2. **Can opinions be measured?**

   Yes, opinions can be measured. In fact, surveys often ask for people's opinions on a topic. But there is no way to know whether or not an opinion is the truth.

HOW TO DIFFERENTIATE FACT FROM OPINION

Human Activities and the Environment

Unfortunately, human use of fossil fuels is one of the most significant developments of the past few centuries. Humans rely on fossil fuels, a non-renewable energy resource, for more than 90 percent of their energy needs.

This careless misuse of our planet's resources has resulted in pollution, global warming, and the destruction of fragile ecosystems. For example, oil pipelines carry more than one million barrels of oil each day across tundra regions. Transporting oil across such areas can only result in oil spills that poison the land for decades.

Opinions
Notice words or phrases that express beliefs or feelings. The words *unfortunately* and *careless* show that opinions are being expressed.

Opinion
Look for statements that speculate about events. These statements are opinions, because they cannot be proved.

Facts
Statements that contain statistics tend to be facts. Writers often use facts to support their opinions.

Lab Handbook

Safety Rules

Before you work in the laboratory, read these safety rules twice. Ask your teacher to explain any rules that you do not completely understand. Refer to these rules later on if you have questions about safety in the science classroom.

Directions

- Read all directions and make sure that you understand them before starting an investigation or lab activity. If you do not understand how to do a procedure or how to use a piece of equipment, ask your teacher.
- Do not begin any investigation or touch any equipment until your teacher has told you to start.
- Never experiment on your own. If you want to try a procedure that the directions do not call for, ask your teacher for permission first.
- If you are hurt or injured in any way, tell your teacher immediately.

Dress Code

goggles

apron

gloves

- Wear goggles when
    — using glassware, sharp objects, or chemicals
    — heating an object
    — working with anything that can easily fly up into the air and hurt someone's eye
- Tie back long hair or hair that hangs in front of your eyes.
- Remove any article of clothing—such as a loose sweater or a scarf—that hangs down and may touch a flame, chemical, or piece of equipment.
- Observe all safety icons calling for the wearing of eye protection, gloves, and aprons.

Heating and Fire Safety

fire
safety

heating
safety

- Keep your work area neat, clean, and free of extra materials.
- Never reach over a flame or heat source.
- Point objects being heated away from you and others.
- Never heat a substance or an object in a closed container.
- Never touch an object that has been heated. If you are unsure whether something is hot, treat it as though it is. Use oven mitts, clamps, tongs, or a test-tube holder.
- Know where the fire extinguisher and fire blanket are kept in your classroom.
- Do not throw hot substances into the trash. Wait for them to cool or use the container your teacher puts out for disposal.

Electrical Safety

electrical safety

- Never use lamps or other electrical equipment with frayed cords.
- Make sure no cord is lying on the floor where someone can trip over it.
- Do not let a cord hang over the side of a counter or table so that the equipment can easily be pulled or knocked to the floor.
- Never let cords hang into sinks or other places where water can be found.
- Never try to fix electrical problems. Inform your teacher of any problems immediately.
- Unplug an electrical cord by pulling on the plug, not the cord.

Chemical Safety

chemical safety

poison

fumes

- If you spill a chemical or get one on your skin or in your eyes, tell your teacher right away.
- Never touch, taste, or sniff any chemicals in the lab. If you need to determine odor, waft. Wafting consists of holding the chemical in its container 15 centimeters (6 in.) away from your nose, and using your fingers to bring fumes from the container to your nose.
- Keep lids on all chemicals you are not using.
- Never put unused chemicals back into the original containers. Throw away extra chemicals where your teacher tells you to.
- Pour chemicals over a sink or your work area, not over the floor.
- If you get a chemical in your eye, use the eyewash right away.
- Always wash your hands after handling chemicals, plants, or soil.

Wafting

Glassware and Sharp-Object Safety

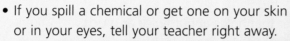

sharp objects

- If you break glassware, tell your teacher right away.
- Do not use broken or chipped glassware. Give these to your teacher.
- Use knives and other cutting instruments carefully. Always wear eye protection and cut away from you.

Animal Safety

- Never hurt an animal.
- Touch animals only when necessary. Follow your teacher's instructions for handling animals.
- Always wash your hands after working with animals.

Cleanup

disposal

- Follow your teacher's instructions for throwing away or putting away supplies.
- Clean your work area and pick up anything that has dropped to the floor.
- Wash your hands.

Using Lab Equipment

Different experiments require different types of equipment. But even though experiments differ, the ways in which the equipment is used are the same.

Beakers

- Use beakers for holding and pouring liquids.
- Do not use a beaker to measure the volume of a liquid. Use a graduated cylinder instead. (See page R16.)
- Use a beaker that holds about twice as much liquid as you need. For example, if you need 100 milliliters of water, you should use a 200- or 250-milliliter beaker.

Test Tubes

- Use test tubes to hold small amounts of substances.
- Do not use a test tube to measure the volume of a liquid.
- Use a test tube when heating a substance over a flame. Aim the mouth of the tube away from yourself and other people.
- Liquids easily spill or splash from test tubes, so it is important to use only small amounts of liquids.

Test-Tube Holder

- Use a test-tube holder when heating a substance in a test tube.
- Use a test-tube holder if the substance in a test tube is dangerous to touch.
- Make sure the test-tube holder tightly grips the test tube so that the test tube will not slide out of the holder.
- Make sure that the test-tube holder is above the surface of the substance in the test tube so that you can observe the substance.

Test-Tube Rack

- Use a test-tube rack to organize test tubes before, during, and after an experiment.

- Use a test-tube rack to keep test tubes upright so that they do not fall over and spill their contents.

- Use a test-tube rack that is the correct size for the test tubes that you are using. If the rack is too small, a test tube may become stuck. If the rack is too large, a test tube may lean over, and some of its contents may spill or splash.

Forceps

- Use forceps when you need to pick up or hold a very small object that should not be touched with your hands.

- Do not use forceps to hold anything over a flame, because forceps are not long enough to keep your hand safely away from the flame. Plastic forceps will melt, and metal forceps will conduct heat and burn your hand.

Hot Plate

- Use a hot plate when a substance needs to be kept warmer than room temperature for a long period of time.

- Use a hot plate instead of a Bunsen burner or a candle when you need to carefully control temperature.

- Do not use a hot plate when a substance needs to be burned in an experiment.

- Always use "hot hands" safety mitts or oven mitts when handling anything that has been heated on a hot plate.

Microscope

Scientists use microscopes to see very small objects that cannot easily be seen with the eye alone. A microscope magnifies the image of an object so that small details may be observed. A microscope that you may use can magnify an object 400 times—the object will appear 400 times larger than its actual size.

LAB HANDBOOK

Body The body separates the lens in the eyepiece from the objective lenses below.

Nosepiece The nosepiece holds the objective lenses above the stage and rotates so that all lenses may be used.

High-Power Objective Lens This is the largest lens on the nosepiece. It magnifies an image approximately 40 times.

Stage The stage supports the object being viewed.

Diaphragm The diaphragm is used to adjust the amount of light passing through the slide and into an objective lens.

Mirror or Light Source Some microscopes use light that is reflected through the stage by a mirror. Other microscopes have their own light sources.

Eyepiece Objects are viewed through the eyepiece. The eyepiece contains a lens that commonly magnifies an image 10 times.

Coarse Adjustment This knob is used to focus the image of an object when it is viewed through the low-power lens.

Fine Adjustment This knob is used to focus the image of an object when it is viewed through the high-power lens.

Low-Power Objective Lens This is the smallest lens on the nosepiece. It magnifies an image approximately 10 times.

Arm The arm supports the body above the stage. Always carry a microscope by the arm and base.

Stage Clip The stage clip holds a slide in place on the stage.

Base The base supports the microscope.

VIEWING AN OBJECT

1. Use the coarse adjustment knob to raise the body tube.

2. Adjust the diaphragm so that you can see a bright circle of light through the eyepiece.

3. Place the object or slide on the stage. Be sure that it is centered over the hole in the stage.

4. Turn the nosepiece to click the low-power lens into place.

5. Using the coarse adjustment knob, slowly lower the lens and focus on the specimen being viewed. Be sure not to touch the slide or object with the lens.

6. When switching from the low-power lens to the high-power lens, first raise the body tube with the coarse adjustment knob so that the high-power lens will not hit the slide.

7. Turn the nosepiece to click the high-power lens into place.

8. Use the fine adjustment knob to focus on the specimen being viewed. Again, be sure not to touch the slide or object with the lens.

MAKING A SLIDE, OR WET MOUNT

1 Place the specimen in the center of a clean slide.

2 Place a drop of water on the specimen.

3 Place a cover slip on the slide. Put one edge of the cover slip into the drop of water and slowly lower it over the specimen.

4 Remove any air bubbles from under the cover slip by gently tapping the cover slip.

5 Dry any excess water before placing the slide on the microscope stage for viewing.

Spring Scale (Force Meter)

- Use a spring scale to measure a force pulling on the scale.

- Use a spring scale to measure the force of gravity exerted on an object by Earth.

- To measure a force accurately, a spring scale must be zeroed before it is used. The scale is zeroed when no weight is attached and the indicator is positioned at zero.

- Do not attach a weight that is either too heavy or too light to a spring scale. A weight that is too heavy could break the scale or exert too great a force for the scale to measure. A weight that is too light may not exert enough force to be measured accurately.

Graduated Cylinder

- Use a graduated cylinder to measure the volume of a liquid.

- Be sure that the graduated cylinder is on a flat surface so that your measurement will be accurate.

- When reading the scale on a graduated cylinder, be sure to have your eyes at the level of the surface of the liquid.

- The surface of the liquid will be curved in the graduated cylinder. Read the volume of the liquid at the bottom of the curve, or meniscus (muh-NIHS-kuhs).

- You can use a graduated cylinder to find the volume of a solid object by measuring the increase in a liquid's level after you add the object to the cylinder.

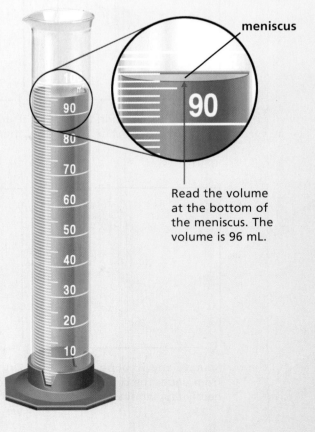

meniscus

Read the volume at the bottom of the meniscus. The volume is 96 mL.

Metric Rulers

- Use metric rulers or meter sticks to measure objects' lengths.

- Do not measure an object from the end of a metric ruler or meter stick, because the end is often imperfect. Instead, measure from the 1-centimeter mark, but remember to subtract a centimeter from the apparent measurement.

- Estimate any lengths that extend between marked units. For example, if a meter stick shows centimeters but not millimeters, you can estimate the length that an object extends between centimeter marks to measure it to the nearest millimeter.

- **Controlling Variables** If you are taking repeated measurements, always measure from the same point each time. For example, if you're measuring how high two different balls bounce when dropped from the same height, measure both bounces at the same point on the balls—either the top or the bottom. Do not measure at the top of one ball and the bottom of the other.

EXAMPLE

How to Measure a Leaf

1. Lay a ruler flat on top of the leaf so that the 1-centimeter mark lines up with one end. Make sure the ruler and the leaf do not move between the time you line them up and the time you take the measurement.

2. Look straight down on the ruler so that you can see exactly how the marks line up with the other end of the leaf.

3. Estimate the length by which the leaf extends beyond a marking. For example, the leaf below extends about halfway between the 4.2-centimeter and 4.3-centimeter marks, so the apparent measurement is about 4.25 centimeters.

4. Remember to subtract 1 centimeter from your apparent measurement, since you started at the 1-centimeter mark on the ruler and not at the end. The leaf is about 3.25 centimeters long (4.25 cm – 1 cm = 3.25 cm).

Triple-Beam Balance

This balance has a pan and three beams with sliding masses, called riders. At one end of the beams is a pointer that indicates whether the mass on the pan is equal to the masses shown on the beams.

1. Make sure the balance is zeroed before measuring the mass of an object. The balance is zeroed if the pointer is at zero when nothing is on the pan and the riders are at their zero points. Use the adjustment knob at the base of the balance to zero it.

2. Place the object to be measured on the pan.

3. Move the riders one notch at a time away from the pan. Begin with the largest rider. If moving the largest rider one notch brings the pointer below zero, begin measuring the mass of the object with the next smaller rider.

4. Change the positions of the riders until they balance the mass on the pan and the pointer is at zero. Then add the readings from the three beams to determine the mass of the object.

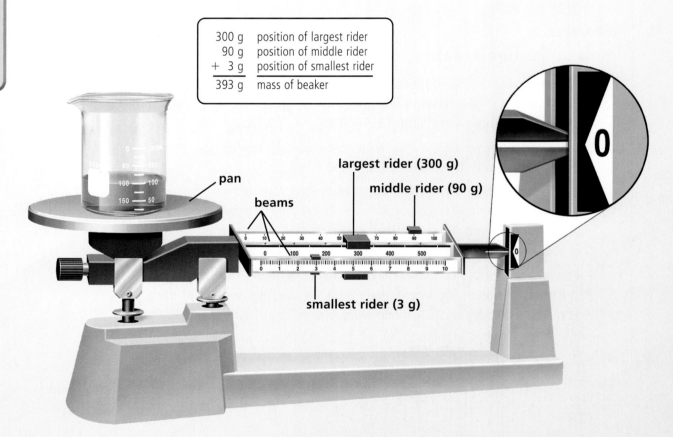

300 g	position of largest rider
90 g	position of middle rider
+ 3 g	position of smallest rider
393 g	mass of beaker

largest rider (300 g)

middle rider (90 g)

pan

beams

smallest rider (3 g)

Double-Pan Balance

This type of balance has two pans. Between the pans is a pointer that indicates whether the masses on the pans are equal.

1. Make sure the balance is zeroed before measuring the mass of an object. The balance is zeroed if the pointer is at zero when there is nothing on either of the pans. Many double-pan balances have sliding knobs that can be used to zero them.

2. Place the object to be measured on one of the pans.

3. Begin adding standard masses to the other pan. Begin with the largest standard mass. If this adds too much mass to the balance, begin measuring the mass of the object with the next smaller standard mass.

4. Add standard masses until the masses on both pans are balanced and the pointer is at zero. Then add the standard masses together to determine the mass of the object being measured.

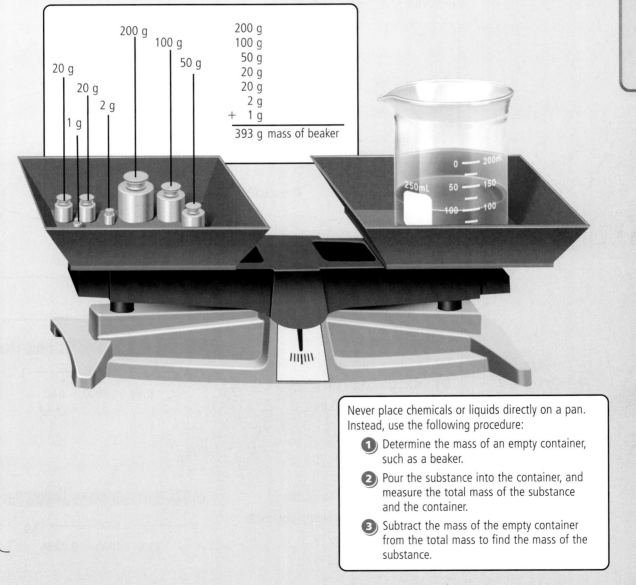

```
        200 g
        100 g
         50 g
         20 g
         20 g
          2 g
     +    1 g
     ─────────────
        393 g  mass of beaker
```

Never place chemicals or liquids directly on a pan. Instead, use the following procedure:

1. Determine the mass of an empty container, such as a beaker.

2. Pour the substance into the container, and measure the total mass of the substance and the container.

3. Subtract the mass of the empty container from the total mass to find the mass of the substance.

The Metric System and SI Units

Scientists use International System (SI) units for measurements of distance, volume, mass, and temperature. The International System is based on multiples of ten and the metric system of measurement.

Basic SI Units		
Property	**Name**	**Symbol**
length	meter	m
volume	liter	L
mass	kilogram	kg
temperature	kelvin	K

SI Prefixes		
Prefix	**Symbol**	**Multiple of 10**
kilo-	k	1000
hecto-	h	100
deca-	da	10
deci-	d	$0.1 \left(\frac{1}{10}\right)$
centi-	c	$0.01 \left(\frac{1}{100}\right)$
milli-	m	$0.001 \left(\frac{1}{1000}\right)$

Changing Metric Units

You can change from one unit to another in the metric system by multiplying or dividing by a power of 10.

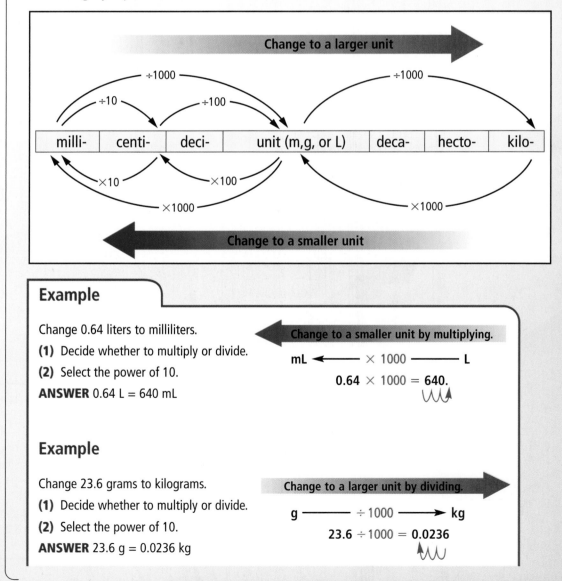

Example

Change 0.64 liters to milliliters.

(1) Decide whether to multiply or divide.

(2) Select the power of 10.

ANSWER 0.64 L = 640 mL

Change to a smaller unit by multiplying.

mL ◄——— × 1000 ——— L

0.64 × 1000 = **640.**

Example

Change 23.6 grams to kilograms.

(1) Decide whether to multiply or divide.

(2) Select the power of 10.

ANSWER 23.6 g = 0.0236 kg

Change to a larger unit by dividing.

g ——— ÷ 1000 ——► kg

23.6 ÷ 1000 = **0.0236**

Temperature Conversions

Even though the kelvin is the SI base unit of temperature, the degree Celsius will be the unit you use most often in your science studies. The formulas below show the relationships between temperatures in degrees Fahrenheit (°F), degrees Celsius (°C), and kelvins (K).

$$°C = \frac{5}{9}(°F - 32)$$

$$°F = \frac{9}{5}°C + 32$$

$$K = °C + 273$$

See page R42 for help with using formulas.

Examples of Temperature Conversions

Condition	Degrees Celsius	Degrees Fahrenheit
Freezing point of water	0	32
Cool day	10	50
Mild day	20	68
Warm day	30	86
Normal body temperature	37	98.6
Very hot day	40	104
Boiling point of water	100	212

Converting Between SI and U.S. Customary Units

Use the chart below when you need to convert between SI units and U.S. customary units.

SI Unit	From SI to U.S. Customary			From U.S. Customary to SI		
Length	When you know	multiply by	to find	When you know	multiply by	to find
kilometer (km) = 1000 m	kilometers	0.62	miles	miles	1.61	kilometers
meter (m) = 100 cm	meters	3.28	feet	feet	0.3048	meters
centimeter (cm) = 10 mm	centimeters	0.39	inches	inches	2.54	centimeters
millimeter (mm) = 0.1 cm	millimeters	0.04	inches	inches	25.4	millimeters
Area	When you know	multiply by	to find	When you know	multiply by	to find
square kilometer (km²)	square kilometers	0.39	square miles	square miles	2.59	square kilometers
square meter (m²)	square meters	1.2	square yards	square yards	0.84	square meters
square centimeter (cm²)	square centimeters	0.155	square inches	square inches	6.45	square centimeters
Volume	When you know	multiply by	to find	When you know	multiply by	to find
liter (L) = 1000 mL	liters	1.06	quarts	quarts	0.95	liters
	liters	0.26	gallons	gallons	3.79	liters
	liters	4.23	cups	cups	0.24	liters
	liters	2.12	pints	pints	0.47	liters
milliliter (mL) = 0.001 L	milliliters	0.20	teaspoons	teaspoons	4.93	milliliters
	milliliters	0.07	tablespoons	tablespoons	14.79	milliliters
	milliliters	0.03	fluid ounces	fluid ounces	29.57	milliliters
Mass	When you know	multiply by	to find	When you know	multiply by	to find
kilogram (kg) = 1000 g	kilograms	2.2	pounds	pounds	0.45	kilograms
gram (g) = 1000 mg	grams	0.035	ounces	ounces	28.35	grams

Precision and Accuracy

When you do an experiment, it is important that your methods, observations, and data be both precise and accurate.

low precision

precision, but not accuracy

precision and accuracy

Precision

In science, **precision** is the exactness and consistency of measurements. For example, measurements made with a ruler that has both centimeter and millimeter markings would be more precise than measurements made with a ruler that has only centimeter markings. Another indicator of precision is the care taken to make sure that methods and observations are as exact and consistent as possible. Every time a particular experiment is done, the same procedure should be used. Precision is necessary because experiments are repeated several times and if the procedure changes, the results will change.

EXAMPLE

Suppose you are measuring temperatures over a two-week period. Your precision will be greater if you measure each temperature at the same place, at the same time of day, and with the same thermometer than if you change any of these factors from one day to the next.

Accuracy

In science, it is possible to be precise but not accurate. **Accuracy** depends on the difference between a measurement and an actual value. The smaller the difference, the more accurate the measurement.

EXAMPLE

Suppose you look at a stream and estimate that it is about 1 meter wide at a particular place. You decide to check your estimate by measuring the stream with a meter stick, and you determine that the stream is 1.32 meters wide. However, because it is hard to measure the width of a stream with a meter stick, it turns out that you didn't do a very good job. The stream is actually 1.14 meters wide. Therefore, even though your estimate was less precise than your measurement, your estimate was actually more accurate.

Making Data Tables and Graphs

Data tables and graphs are useful tools for both recording and communicating scientific data.

Making Data Tables

You can use a **data table** to organize and record the measurements that you make. Some examples of information that might be recorded in data tables are frequencies, times, and amounts.

EXAMPLE

Suppose you are investigating photosynthesis in two elodea plants. One sits in direct sunlight, and the other sits in a dimly lit room. You measure the rate of photosynthesis by counting the number of bubbles in the jar every ten minutes.

1. Title and number your data table.
2. Decide how you will organize the table into columns and rows.
3. Any units, such as seconds or degrees, should be included in column headings, not in the individual cells.

Table 1. Number of Bubbles from Elodea

Time (min)	Sunlight	Dim Light
0	0	0
10	15	5
20	25	8
30	32	7
40	41	10
50	47	9
60	42	9

> Always number and title data tables.

The data in the table above could also be organized in a different way.

Table 1. Number of Bubbles from Elodea

Light Condition	Time (min)						
	0	10	20	30	40	50	60
Sunlight	0	15	25	32	41	47	42
Dim light	0	5	8	7	10	9	9

> Put units in column heading.

Making Line Graphs

You can use a **line graph** to show a relationship between variables. Line graphs are particularly useful for showing changes in variables over time.

EXAMPLE

Suppose you are interested in graphing temperature data that you collected over the course of a day.

Table 1. Outside Temperature During the Day on March 7

	Time of Day						
	7:00 A.M.	9:00 A.M.	11:00 A.M.	1:00 P.M.	3:00 P.M.	5:00 P.M.	7:00 P.M.
Temp (°C)	8	9	11	14	12	10	6

1. Use the vertical axis of your line graph for the variable that you are measuring—temperature.

2. Choose scales for both the horizontal axis and the vertical axis of the graph. You should have two points more than you need on the vertical axis, and the horizontal axis should be long enough for all of the data points to fit.

3. Draw and label each axis.

4. Graph each value. First find the appropriate point on the scale of the horizontal axis. Imagine a line that rises vertically from that place on the scale. Then find the corresponding value on the vertical axis, and imagine a line that moves horizontally from that value. The point where these two imaginary lines intersect is where the value should be plotted.

5. Connect the points with straight lines.

Be sure to add a number and a title to your graph.

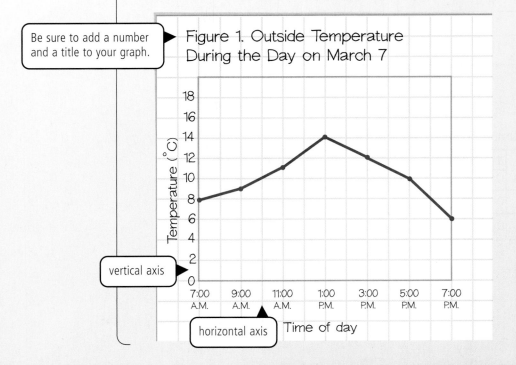

Figure 1. Outside Temperature During the Day on March 7

vertical axis

horizontal axis

Time of day

Making Circle Graphs

You can use a **circle graph,** sometimes called a pie chart, to represent data as parts of a circle. Circle graphs are used only when the data can be expressed as percentages of a whole. The entire circle shown in a circle graph is equal to 100 percent of the data.

EXAMPLE

Suppose you identified the species of each mature tree growing in a small wooded area. You organized your data in a table, but you also want to show the data in a circle graph.

1. To begin, find the total number of mature trees.

    $56 + 34 + 22 + 10 + 28 = 150$

2. To find the degree measure for each sector of the circle, write a fraction comparing the number of each tree species with the total number of trees. Then multiply the fraction by 360°.

    Oak: $\dfrac{56}{150} \times 360° = 134.4°$

3. Draw a circle. Use a protractor to draw the angle for each sector of the graph.

4. Color and label each sector of the graph.

5. Give the graph a number and title.

Table 1. Tree Species in Wooded Area

Species	Number of Specimens
Oak	56
Maple	34
Birch	22
Willow	10
Pine	28

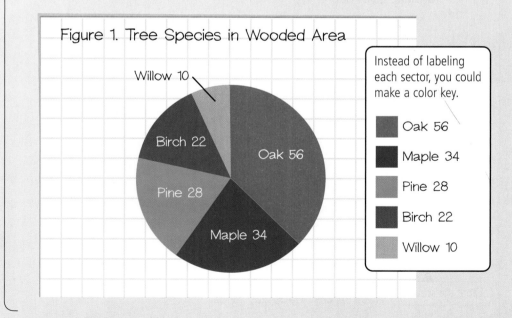

Figure 1. Tree Species in Wooded Area

Willow 10
Birch 22
Pine 28
Oak 56
Maple 34

Instead of labeling each sector, you could make a color key.

- Oak 56
- Maple 34
- Pine 28
- Birch 22
- Willow 10

Bar Graph

A **bar graph** is a type of graph in which the lengths of the bars are used to represent and compare data. A numerical scale is used to determine the lengths of the bars.

EXAMPLE

To determine the effect of water on seed sprouting, three cups were filled with sand, and ten seeds were planted in each. Different amounts of water were added to each cup over a three-day period.

Table 1. Effect of Water on Seed Sprouting

Daily Amount of Water (mL)	Number of Seeds That Sprouted After 3 Days in Sand
0	1
10	4
20	8

1. Choose a numerical scale. The greatest value is 8, so the end of the scale should have a value greater than 8, such as 10. Use equal increments along the scale, such as increments of 2.

2. Draw and label the axes. Mark intervals on the vertical axis according to the scale you chose.

3. Draw a bar for each data value. Use the scale to decide how long to make each bar.

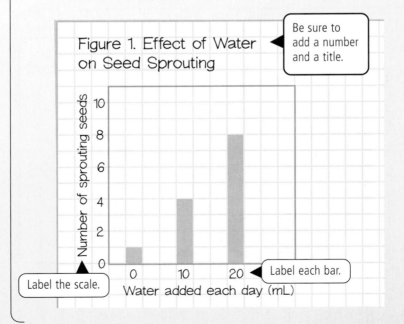

Figure 1. Effect of Water on Seed Sprouting

Be sure to add a number and a title.

Label the scale.

Label each bar.

Double Bar Graph

A **double bar graph** is a bar graph that shows two sets of data. The two bars for each measurement are drawn next to each other.

EXAMPLE

The seed-sprouting experiment was done using both sand and potting soil. The data for sand and potting soil can be plotted on one graph.

1. Draw one set of bars, using the data for sand, as shown below.

2. Draw bars for the potting-soil data next to the bars for the sand data. Shade them a different color. Add a key.

Table 2. Effect of Water and Soil on Seed Sprouting

Daily Amount of Water (mL)	Number of Seeds That Sprouted After 3 Days in Sand	Number of Seeds That Sprouted After 3 Days in Potting Soil
0	1	2
10	4	5
20	8	9

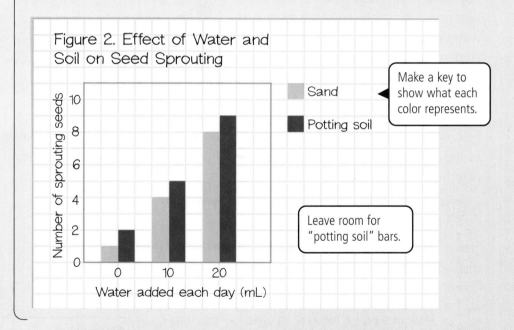

Figure 2. Effect of Water and Soil on Seed Sprouting

Make a key to show what each color represents.

Leave room for "potting soil" bars.

Designing an Experiment

Use this section when designing or conducting an experiment.

Determining a Purpose

You can find a purpose for an experiment by doing research, by examining the results of a previous experiment, or by observing the world around you. An **experiment** is an organized procedure to study something under controlled conditions.

> Don't forget to learn as much as possible about your topic before you begin.

1. Write the purpose of your experiment as a question or problem that you want to investigate.

2. Write down research questions and begin searching for information that will help you design an experiment. Consult the library, the Internet, and other people as you conduct your research.

EXAMPLE

Middle school students observed an odor near the lake by their school. They also noticed that the water on the side of the lake near the school was greener than the water on the other side of the lake. The students did some research to learn more about their observations. They discovered that the odor and green color in the lake came from algae. They also discovered that a new fertilizer was being used on a field nearby. The students inferred that the use of the fertilizer might be related to the presence of the algae and designed a controlled experiment to find out whether they were right.

Problem

How does fertilizer affect the presence of algae in a lake?

Research Questions

- Have other experiments been done on this problem? If so, what did those experiments show?

- What kind of fertilizer is used on the field? How much?

- How do algae grow?

- How do people measure algae?

- Can fertilizer and algae be used safely in a lab? How?

> **Research**
> As you research, you may find a topic that is more interesting to you than your original topic, or learn that a procedure you wanted to use is not practical or safe. It is OK to change your purpose as you research.

Writing a Hypothesis

A **hypothesis** is a tentative explanation for an observation or scientific problem that can be tested by further investigation. You can write your hypothesis in the form of an "If . . . , then . . . , because . . ." statement.

Hypothesis

If the amount of fertilizer in lake water is increased, then the amount of algae will also increase, because fertilizers provide nutrients that algae need to grow.

Hypotheses
For help with hypotheses, refer to page R3.

Determining Materials

Make a list of all the materials you will need to do your experiment. Be specific, especially if someone else is helping you obtain the materials. Try to think of everything you will need.

Materials

- 1 large jar or container
- 4 identical smaller containers
- rubber gloves that also cover the arms
- sample of fertilizer-and-water solution
- eyedropper
- clear plastic wrap
- scissors
- masking tape
- marker
- ruler

Determining Variables and Constants

EXPERIMENTAL GROUP AND CONTROL GROUP

An experiment to determine how two factors are related always has two groups—a control group and an experimental group.

1. Design an experimental group. Include as many trials as possible in the experimental group in order to obtain reliable results.

2. Design a control group that is the same as the experimental group in every way possible, except for the factor you wish to test.

Experimental Group: two containers of lake water with one drop of fertilizer solution added to each

Control Group: two containers of lake water with no fertilizer solution added

> Go back to your materials list and make sure you have enough items listed to cover both your experimental group and your control group.

VARIABLES AND CONSTANTS

Identify the variables and constants in your experiment. In a controlled experiment, a **variable** is any factor that can change. **Constants** are all of the factors that are the same in both the experimental group and the control group.

1. Read your hypothesis. The **independent variable** is the factor that you wish to test and that is manipulated or changed so that it can be tested. The independent variable is expressed in your hypothesis after the word *if*. Identify the independent variable in your laboratory report.

2. The **dependent variable** is the factor that you measure to gather results. It is expressed in your hypothesis after the word *then*. Identify the dependent variable in your laboratory report.

Hypothesis
If the amount of fertilizer in lake water is increased, then the amount of algae will also increase, because fertilizers provide nutrients that algae need to grow.

Table 1. Variables and Constants in Algae Experiment

Independent Variable	Dependent Variable	Constants
Amount of fertilizer in lake water	Amount of algae that grow	• Where the lake water is obtained • Type of container used • Light and temperature conditions where water will be stored

> Set up your experiment so that you will test only one variable.

MEASURING THE DEPENDENT VARIABLE

Before starting your experiment, you need to define how you will measure the dependent variable. An **operational definition** is a description of the one particular way in which you will measure the dependent variable.

Your operational definition is important for several reasons. First, in any experiment there are several ways in which a dependent variable can be measured. Second, the procedure of the experiment depends on how you decide to measure the dependent variable. Third, your operational definition makes it possible for other people to evaluate and build on your experiment.

EXAMPLE 1

An operational definition of a dependent variable can be qualitative. That is, your measurement of the dependent variable can simply be an observation of whether a change occurs as a result of a change in the independent variable. This type of operational definition can be thought of as a "yes or no" measurement.

Table 2. Qualitative Operational Definition of Algae Growth

Independent Variable	Dependent Variable	Operational Definition
Amount of fertilizer in lake water	Amount of algae that grow	Algae grow in lake water

A qualitative measurement of a dependent variable is often easy to make and record. However, this type of information does not provide a great deal of detail in your experimental results.

EXAMPLE 2

An operational definition of a dependent variable can be quantitative. That is, your measurement of the dependent variable can be a number that shows how much change occurs as a result of a change in the independent variable.

Table 3. Quantitative Operational Definition of Algae Growth

Independent Variable	Dependent Variable	Operational Definition
Amount of fertilizer in lake water	Amount of algae that grow	Diameter of largest algal growth (in mm)

A quantitative measurement of a dependent variable can be more difficult to make and analyze than a qualitative measurement. However, this type of data provides much more information about your experiment and is often more useful.

Writing a Procedure

Write each step of your procedure. Start each step with a verb, or action word, and keep the steps short. Your procedure should be clear enough for someone else to use as instructions for repeating your experiment.

> If necessary, go back to your materials list and add any materials that you left out.

Procedure

1. Put on your gloves. Use the large container to obtain a sample of lake water.

2. Divide the sample of lake water equally among the four smaller containers.

> **Controlling Variables**
> The same amount of fertilizer solution must be added to two of the four containers.

3. Use the eyedropper to add one drop of fertilizer solution to two of the containers.

4. Use the masking tape and the marker to label the containers with your initials, the date, and the identifiers "Jar 1 with Fertilizer," "Jar 2 with Fertilizer," "Jar 1 without Fertilizer," and "Jar 2 without Fertilizer."

5. Cover the containers with clear plastic wrap. Use the scissors to punch ten holes in each of the covers.

> **Controlling Variables**
> All four containers must receive the same amount of light.

6. Place all four containers on a window ledge. Make sure that they all receive the same amount of light.

7. Observe the containers every day for one week.

8. Use the ruler to measure the diameter of the largest clump of algae in each container, and record your measurements daily.

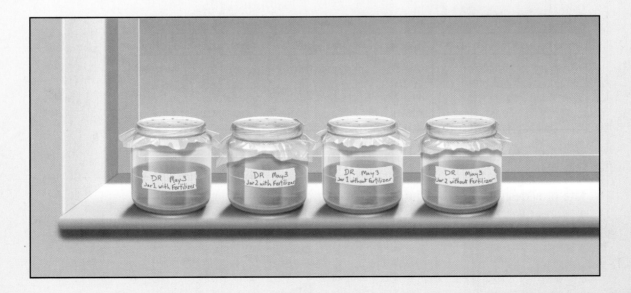

Recording Observations

Once you have obtained all of your materials and your procedure has been approved, you can begin making experimental observations. Gather both quantitative and qualitative data. If something goes wrong during your procedure, make sure you record that too.

Observations
For help with making qualitative and quantitative observations, refer to page R2.

For more examples of data tables, see page R23.

Table 4. Fertilizer and Algae Growth

| Date and Time | Experimental Group | | Control Group | | |
	Jar 1 with Fertilizer (diameter of algae in mm)	Jar 2 with Fertilizer (diameter of algae in mm)	Jar 1 without Fertilizer (diameter of algae in mm)	Jar 2 without Fertilizer (diameter of algae in mm)	Observations
5/3 4:00 P.M.	0	0	0	0	condensation in all containers
5/4 4:00 P.M.	0	3	0	0	tiny green blobs in jar 2 with fertilizer
5/5 4:15 P.M.	4	5	0	3	green blobs in jars 1 and 2 with fertilizer and jar 2 without fertilizer
5/6 4:00 P.M.	5	6	0	4	water light green in jar 2 with fertilizer
5/7 4:00 P.M.	8	10	0	6	water light green in jars 1 and 2 with fertilizer and in jar 2 without fertilizer
5/8 3:30 P.M.	10	18	0	6	cover off jar 2 with fertilizer
5/9 3:30 P.M.	14	23	0	8	drew sketches of each container

Notice that on the sixth day, the observer found that the cover was off one of the containers. It is important to record observations of unintended factors because they might affect the results of the experiment.

Use technology, such as a microscope, to help you make observations when possible.

Drawings of Samples Viewed Under Microscope on 5/9 at 100x

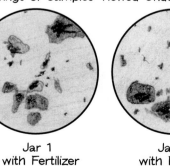
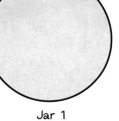
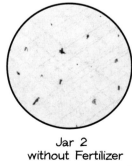

| Jar 1 with Fertilizer | Jar 2 with Fertilizer | Jar 1 without Fertilizer | Jar 2 without Fertilizer |

LAB HANDBOOK

Summarizing Results

To summarize your data, look at all of your observations together. Look for meaningful ways to present your observations. For example, you might average your data or make a graph to look for patterns. When possible, use spreadsheet software to help you analyze and present your data. The two graphs below show the same data.

EXAMPLE 1

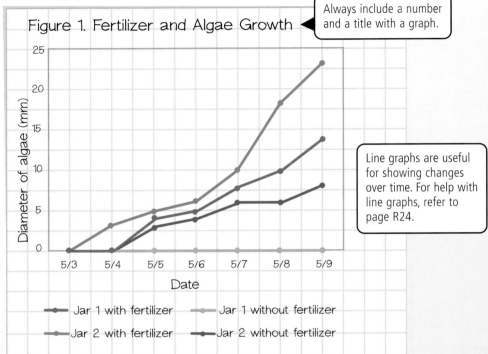

Figure 1. Fertilizer and Algae Growth

> Always include a number and a title with a graph.

> Line graphs are useful for showing changes over time. For help with line graphs, refer to page R24.

EXAMPLE 2

> Bar graphs are useful for comparing different data sets. This bar graph has four bars for each day. Another way to present the data would be to calculate averages for the tests and the controls, and to show one test bar and one control bar for each day.

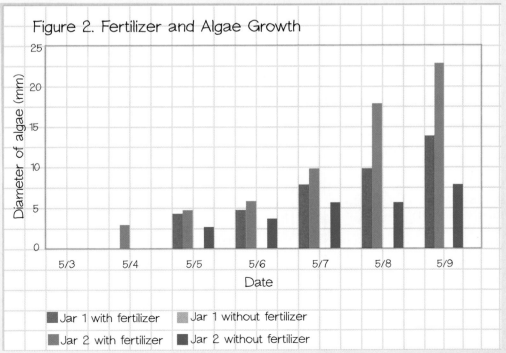

Figure 2. Fertilizer and Algae Growth

Drawing Conclusions

RESULTS AND INFERENCES

To draw conclusions from your experiment, first write your results. Then compare your results with your hypothesis. Do your results support your hypothesis? Be careful not to make inferences about factors that you did not test.

> For help with making inferences, see page R4.

Results and Inferences

The results of my experiment show that more algae grew in lake water to which fertilizer had been added than in lake water to which no fertilizer had been added. My hypothesis was supported. I infer that it is possible that the growth of algae in the lake was caused by the fertilizer used on the field.

> Notice that you cannot conclude from this experiment that the presence of algae in the lake was due only to the fertilizer.

QUESTIONS FOR FURTHER RESEARCH

Write a list of questions for further research and investigation. Your ideas may lead you to new experiments and discoveries.

Questions for Further Research

• What is the connection between the amount of fertilizer and algae growth?

• How do different brands of fertilizer affect algae growth?

• How would algae growth in the lake be affected if no fertilizer were used on the field?

• How do algae affect the lake and the other life in and around it?

• How does fertilizer affect the lake and the life in and around it?

• If fertilizer is getting into the lake, how is it getting there?

Math Handbook

Describing a Set of Data

Means, medians, modes, and ranges are important math tools for describing data sets such as the following widths of fossilized clamshells.

13 mm   25 mm   14 mm   21 mm   16 mm   23 mm   14 mm

Mean

The **mean** of a data set is the sum of the values divided by the number of values.

> **Example**
>
> To find the mean of the clamshell data, add the values and then divide the sum by the number of values.
>
> $$\frac{13\ mm + 25\ mm + 14\ mm + 21\ mm + 16\ mm + 23\ mm + 14\ mm}{7} = \frac{126\ mm}{7} = 18\ mm$$
>
> **ANSWER** The mean is 18 mm.

Median

The **median** of a data set is the middle value when the values are written in numerical order. If a data set has an even number of values, the median is the mean of the two middle values.

> **Example**
>
> To find the median of the clamshell data, arrange the values in order from least to greatest. The median is the middle value.
>
> 13 mm   14 mm   14 mm   16 mm   21 mm   23 mm   25 mm
>
> **ANSWER** The median is 16 mm.

Mode

The **mode** of a data set is the value that occurs most often.

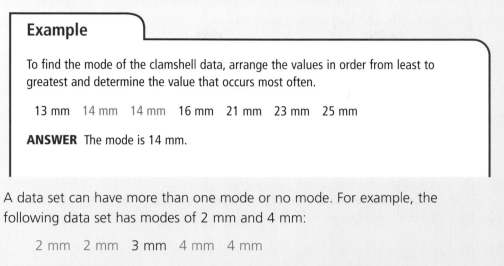

> ### Example
>
> To find the mode of the clamshell data, arrange the values in order from least to greatest and determine the value that occurs most often.
>
> 13 mm   14 mm   14 mm   16 mm   21 mm   23 mm   25 mm
>
> **ANSWER** The mode is 14 mm.

A data set can have more than one mode or no mode. For example, the following data set has modes of 2 mm and 4 mm:

2 mm   2 mm   3 mm   4 mm   4 mm

The data set below has no mode, because no value occurs more often than any other.

2 mm   3 mm   4 mm   5 mm

Range

The **range** of a data set is the difference between the greatest value and the least value.

> ### Example
>
> To find the range of the clamshell data, arrange the values in order from least to greatest.
>
> 13 mm   14 mm   14 mm   16 mm   21 mm   23 mm   25 mm
>
> Subtract the least value from the greatest value.
>
> 13 mm is the least value.
> 25 mm is the greatest value.
>
> 25 mm − 13 mm = 12 mm
>
> **ANSWER** The range is 12 mm.

Using Ratios, Rates, and Proportions

You can use ratios and rates to compare values in data sets. You can use proportions to find unknown values.

Ratios

A **ratio** uses division to compare two values. The ratio of a value a to a nonzero value b can be written as $\frac{a}{b}$.

> ### Example
>
> The height of one plant is 8 centimeters. The height of another plant is 6 centimeters. To find the ratio of the height of the first plant to the height of the second plant, write a fraction and simplify it.
>
> $$\frac{8 \text{ cm}}{6 \text{ cm}} = \frac{4 \times \overset{1}{\cancel{2}}}{3 \times \underset{1}{\cancel{2}}} = \frac{4}{3}$$
>
> **ANSWER** The ratio of the plant heights is $\frac{4}{3}$.

You can also write the ratio $\frac{a}{b}$ as "a to b" or as $a:b$. For example, you can write the ratio of the plant heights as "4 to 3" or as 4:3.

Rates

A **rate** is a ratio of two values expressed in different units. A unit rate is a rate with a denominator of 1 unit.

> ### Example
>
> A plant grew 6 centimeters in 2 days. The plant's rate of growth was $\frac{6 \text{ cm}}{2 \text{ days}}$. To describe the plant's growth in centimeters per day, write a unit rate.
>
>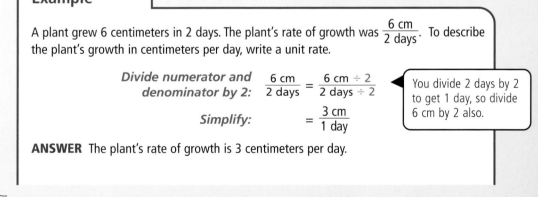
>
> *Divide numerator and denominator by 2:* $\quad \dfrac{6 \text{ cm}}{2 \text{ days}} = \dfrac{6 \text{ cm} \div 2}{2 \text{ days} \div 2}$
>
> You divide 2 days by 2 to get 1 day, so divide 6 cm by 2 also.
>
> *Simplify:* $\quad = \dfrac{3 \text{ cm}}{1 \text{ day}}$
>
> **ANSWER** The plant's rate of growth is 3 centimeters per day.

Proportions

A **proportion** is an equation stating that two ratios are equivalent. To solve for an unknown value in a proportion, you can use cross products.

Example

If a plant grew 6 centimeters in 2 days, how many centimeters would it grow in 3 days (if its rate of growth is constant)?

Write a proportion:	$\dfrac{6 \text{ cm}}{2 \text{ days}} = \dfrac{x}{3 \text{ days}}$
Set cross products:	$6 \text{ cm} \cdot 3 = 2x$
Multiply 6 and 3:	$18 \text{ cm} = 2x$
Divide each side by 2:	$\dfrac{18 \text{ cm}}{2} = \dfrac{2x}{2}$
Simplify:	$9 \text{ cm} = x$

ANSWER The plant would grow 9 centimeters in 3 days.

Using Decimals, Fractions, and Percents

Decimals, fractions, and percentages are all ways of recording and representing data.

Decimals

A **decimal** is a number that is written in the base-ten place value system, in which a decimal point separates the ones and tenths digits. The values of each place is ten times that of the place to its right.

Example

A caterpillar traveled from point *A* to point *C* along the path shown.

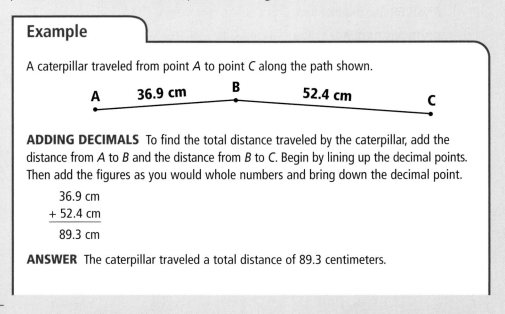

ADDING DECIMALS To find the total distance traveled by the caterpillar, add the distance from *A* to *B* and the distance from *B* to *C*. Begin by lining up the decimal points. Then add the figures as you would whole numbers and bring down the decimal point.

```
  36.9 cm
+ 52.4 cm
  89.3 cm
```

ANSWER The caterpillar traveled a total distance of 89.3 centimeters.

Example *continued*

SUBTRACTING DECIMALS To find how much farther the caterpillar traveled on the second leg of the journey, subtract the distance from *A* to *B* from the distance from *B* to *C*.

$$
\begin{array}{r}
52.4 \text{ cm} \\
- \ 36.9 \text{ cm} \\
\hline
15.5 \text{ cm}
\end{array}
$$

ANSWER The caterpillar traveled 15.5 centimeters farther on the second leg of the journey.

Example

A caterpillar is traveling from point *D* to point *F* along the path shown. The caterpillar travels at a speed of 9.6 centimeters per minute.

MULTIPLYING DECIMALS You can multiply decimals as you would whole numbers. The number of decimal places in the product is equal to the sum of the number of decimal places in the factors.

For instance, suppose it takes the caterpillar 1.5 minutes to go from *D* to *E*. To find the distance from *D* to *E*, multiply the caterpillar's speed by the time it took.

Align as shown.

$$
\begin{array}{rl}
9.6 & 1 \quad \text{decimal place} \\
\times \ 1.5 & + \ 1 \quad \text{decimal place} \\
\hline
480 & \\
96 & \\
\hline
14.40 & 2 \quad \text{decimal places}
\end{array}
$$

ANSWER The distance from *D* to *E* is 14.4 centimeters.

DIVIDING DECIMALS When you divide by a decimal, move the decimal points the same number of places in the divisor and the dividend to make the divisor a whole number.

For instance, to find the time it will take the caterpillar to travel from *E* to *F*, divide the distance from *E* to *F* by the caterpillar's speed.

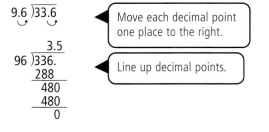

Move each decimal point one place to the right.

Line up decimal points.

ANSWER The caterpillar will travel from *E* to *F* in 3.5 minutes.

Fractions

A **fraction** is a number in the form $\frac{a}{b}$, where b is not equal to 0. A fraction is in **simplest form** if its numerator and denominator have a greatest common factor (GCF) of 1. To simplify a fraction, divide its numerator and denominator by their GCF.

Example

A caterpillar is 40 millimeters long. The head of the caterpillar is 6 millimeters long. To compare the length of the caterpillar's head with the caterpillar's total length, you can write and simplify a fraction that expresses the ratio of the two lengths.

Write the ratio of the two lengths: $\dfrac{\text{Length of head}}{\text{Total length}} = \dfrac{6 \text{ mm}}{40 \text{ mm}}$

Write numerator and denominator as products of numbers and the GCF: $= \dfrac{3 \times 2}{20 \times 2}$

Divide numerator and denominator by the GCF: $= \dfrac{3 \times \overset{1}{\cancel{2}}}{20 \times \underset{1}{\cancel{2}}}$

Simplify: $= \dfrac{3}{20}$

ANSWER In simplest form, the ratio of the lengths is $\dfrac{3}{20}$.

Percents

A **percent** is a ratio that compares a number to 100. The word *percent* means "per hundred" or "out of 100." The symbol for *percent* is %.

For instance, suppose 43 out of 100 caterpillars are female. You can represent this ratio as a percent, a decimal, or a fraction.

Percent	Decimal	Fraction
43%	0.43	$\dfrac{43}{100}$

Example

In the preceding example, the ratio of the length of the caterpillar's head to the caterpillar's total length is $\dfrac{3}{20}$. To write this ratio as a percent, write an equivalent fraction that has a denominator of 100.

Multiply numerator and denominator by 5: $\dfrac{3}{20} = \dfrac{3 \times 5}{20 \times 5}$

$= \dfrac{15}{100}$

Write as a percent: $= 15\%$

ANSWER The caterpillar's head represents 15 percent of its total length.

Using Formulas

A **formula** is an equation that shows the general relationship between two or more quantities.

> The term *variable* is also used in science to refer to a factor that can change during an experiment.

In science, a formula often has a word form and a symbolic form. The formula below expresses Ohm's law.

Word Form

$$\text{Current} = \frac{\text{voltage}}{\text{resistance}}$$

Symbolic Form

$$I = \frac{V}{R}$$

In this formula, I, V, and R are variables. A mathematical **variable** is a symbol or letter that is used to represent one or more numbers.

Example

Suppose that you measure a voltage of 1.5 volts and a resistance of 15 ohms. You can use the formula for Ohm's law to find the current in amperes.

Write the formula for Ohm's law: $\quad I = \dfrac{V}{R}$

Substitute 1.5 volts for V and 15 ohms for R: $\quad I = \dfrac{1.5 \text{ volts}}{15 \text{ ohms}}$

Simplify: $\quad I = 0.1 \text{ amp}$

ANSWER The current is 0.1 ampere.

If you know the values of all variables but one in a formula, you can solve for the value of the unknown variable. For instance, Ohm's law can be used to find a voltage if you know the current and the resistance.

Example

Suppose that you know that a current is 0.2 amperes and the resistance is 18 ohms. Use the formula for Ohm's law to find the voltage in volts.

Write the formula for Ohm's law: $\quad I = \dfrac{V}{R}$

Substitute 0.2 amp for I and 18 ohms for R: $\quad 0.2 \text{ amp} = \dfrac{V}{18 \text{ ohms}}$

Multiply both sides by 18 ohms: $\quad 0.2 \text{ amp} \cdot 18 \text{ ohms} = V$

Simplify: $\quad 3.6 \text{ volts} = V$

ANSWER The voltage is 3.6 volts.

Finding Areas

The area of a figure is the amount of surface the figure covers.

Area is measured in square units, such as square meters (m²) or square centimeters (cm²). Formulas for the areas of three common geometric figures are shown below.

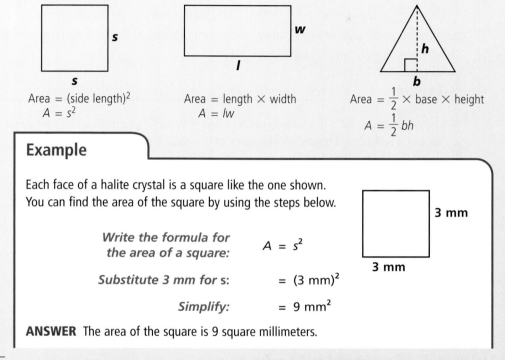

Area = (side length)²
$A = s^2$

Area = length × width
$A = lw$

Area = $\frac{1}{2}$ × base × height

$A = \frac{1}{2} bh$

Example

Each face of a halite crystal is a square like the one shown. You can find the area of the square by using the steps below.

Write the formula for the area of a square: $A = s^2$

Substitute 3 mm for s: = (3 mm)²

Simplify: = 9 mm²

ANSWER The area of the square is 9 square millimeters.

Finding Volumes

The volume of a solid is the amount of space contained by the solid.

Volume is measured in cubic units, such as cubic meters (m³) or cubic centimeters (cm³). The volume of a rectangular prism is given by the formula shown below.

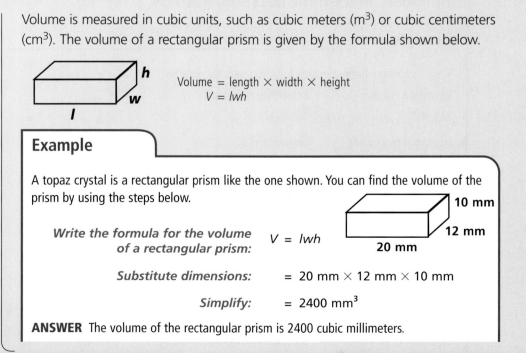

Volume = length × width × height
$V = lwh$

Example

A topaz crystal is a rectangular prism like the one shown. You can find the volume of the prism by using the steps below.

Write the formula for the volume of a rectangular prism: $V = lwh$

Substitute dimensions: = 20 mm × 12 mm × 10 mm

Simplify: = 2400 mm³

ANSWER The volume of the rectangular prism is 2400 cubic millimeters.

Using Significant Figures

The **significant figures** in a decimal are the digits that are warranted by the accuracy of a measuring device.

When you perform a calculation with measurements, the number of significant figures to include in the result depends in part on the number of significant figures in the measurements. When you multiply or divide measurements, your answer should have only as many significant figures as the measurement with the fewest significant figures.

Example

Using a balance and a graduated cylinder filled with water, you determined that a marble has a mass of 8.0 grams and a volume of 3.5 cubic centimeters. To calculate the density of the marble, divide the mass by the volume.

Write the formula for density:	Density $= \dfrac{\text{mass}}{\text{Volume}}$
Substitute measurements:	$= \dfrac{8.0 \text{ g}}{3.5 \text{ cm}^3}$
Use a calculator to divide:	$\approx 2.285714286 \text{ g/cm}^3$

ANSWER Because the mass and the volume have two significant figures each, give the density to two significant figures. The marble has a density of 2.3 grams per cubic centimeter.

Using Scientific Notation

Scientific notation is a shorthand way to write very large or very small numbers. For example, 73,500,000,000,000,000,000,000 kg is the mass of the Moon. In scientific notation, it is 7.35×10^{22} kg.

Example

You can convert from standard form to scientific notation.

Standard Form	Scientific Notation
720,000	7.2×10^5
5 decimal places left	Exponent is 5.
0.000291	2.91×10^{-4}
4 decimal places right	Exponent is −4.

You can convert from scientific notation to standard form.

Scientific Notation	Standard Form
4.63×10^7	46,300,000
Exponent is 7.	7 decimal places right
1.08×10^{-6}	0.00000108
Exponent is −6.	6 decimal places left

Note-Taking Handbook

Note-Taking Strategies

Taking notes as you read helps you understand the information. The notes you take can also be used as a study guide for later review. This handbook presents several ways to organize your notes.

Content Frame

1. Make a chart in which each column represents a category.
2. Give each column a heading.
3. Write details under the headings.

NAME	GROUP	CHARACTERISTICS	DRAWING
snail	mollusks	mantle, shell	
ant	arthropods	six legs, exoskeleton	
earthworm	segmented worms	segmented body, circulatory and digestive systems	
heartworm	roundworms	digestive system	
sea star	echinoderms	spiny skin, tube feet	
jellyfish	cnidarians	stinging cells	

categories

details

Combination Notes

1. For each new idea or concept, write an informal outline of the information.
2. Make a sketch to illustrate the concept, and label it.

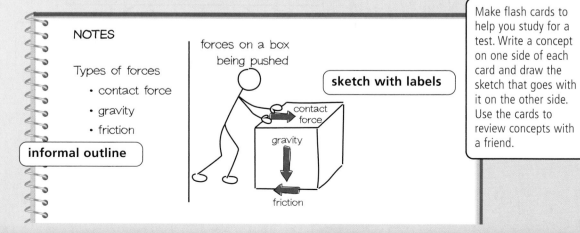

NOTES

Types of forces
- contact force
- gravity
- friction

informal outline

forces on a box being pushed

sketch with labels

contact force

gravity

friction

Make flash cards to help you study for a test. Write a concept on one side of each card and draw the sketch that goes with it on the other side. Use the cards to review concepts with a friend.

Main Idea and Detail Notes

1. In the left-hand column of a two-column chart, list main ideas. The blue headings express main ideas throughout this textbook.

2. In the right-hand column, write details that expand on each main idea.

You can shorten the headings in your chart. Be sure to use the most important words.

When studying for tests, cover up the detail notes column with a sheet of paper. Then use each main idea to form a question—such as "How does latitude affect climate?" Answer the question, and then uncover the detail notes column to check your answer.

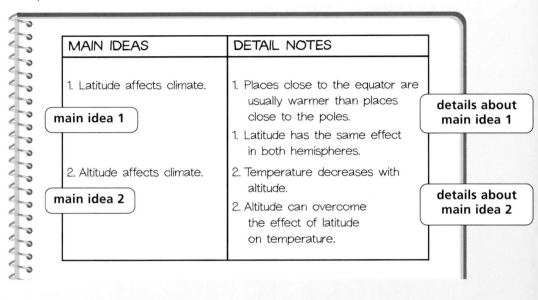

MAIN IDEAS	DETAIL NOTES
1. Latitude affects climate. **main idea 1**	1. Places close to the equator are usually warmer than places close to the poles. 1. Latitude has the same effect in both hemispheres.
2. Altitude affects climate. **main idea 2**	2. Temperature decreases with altitude. 2. Altitude can overcome the effect of latitude on temperature.

details about main idea 1

details about main idea 2

Main Idea Web

1. Write a main idea in a box.

2. Add boxes around it with related vocabulary terms and important details.

You can find definitions near highlighted terms.

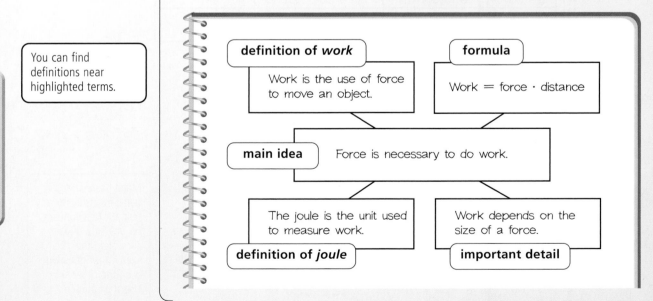

definition of *work*
Work is the use of force to move an object.

formula
Work = force · distance

main idea   Force is necessary to do work.

The joule is the unit used to measure work.
definition of *joule*

Work depends on the size of a force.
important detail

Mind Map

1. Write a main idea in the center.

2. Add details that relate to one another and to the main idea.

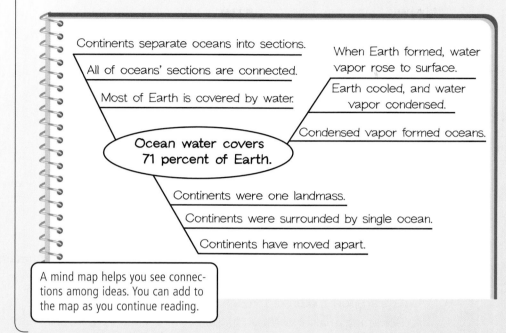

Continents separate oceans into sections.

All of oceans' sections are connected.

Most of Earth is covered by water.

When Earth formed, water vapor rose to surface.

Earth cooled, and water vapor condensed.

Condensed vapor formed oceans.

Ocean water covers 71 percent of Earth.

Continents were one landmass.

Continents were surrounded by single ocean.

Continents have moved apart.

A mind map helps you see connections among ideas. You can add to the map as you continue reading.

Supporting Main Ideas

1. Write a main idea in a box.

2. Add boxes underneath with information—such as reasons, explanations, and examples—that supports the main idea.

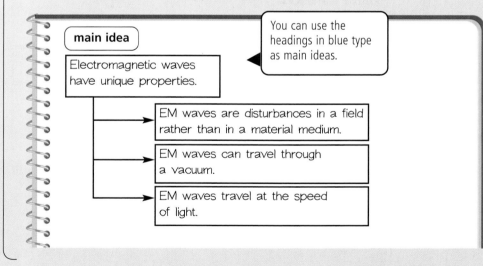

main idea

Electromagnetic waves have unique properties.

You can use the headings in blue type as main ideas.

EM waves are disturbances in a field rather than in a material medium.

EM waves can travel through a vacuum.

EM waves travel at the speed of light.

Outline

1. Copy the chapter title and headings from the book in the form of an outline.

2. Add notes that summarize in your own words what you read.

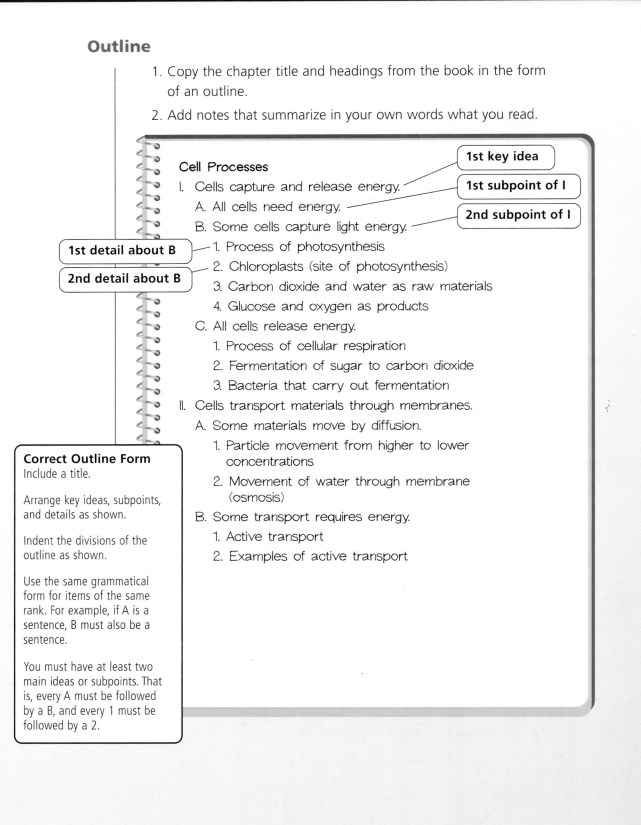

Cell Processes

I. Cells capture and release energy. — **1st key idea**
  A. All cells need energy. — **1st subpoint of I**
  B. Some cells capture light energy. — **2nd subpoint of I**
    1. Process of photosynthesis — **1st detail about B**
    2. Chloroplasts (site of photosynthesis) — **2nd detail about B**
    3. Carbon dioxide and water as raw materials
    4. Glucose and oxygen as products
  C. All cells release energy.
    1. Process of cellular respiration
    2. Fermentation of sugar to carbon dioxide
    3. Bacteria that carry out fermentation
II. Cells transport materials through membranes.
  A. Some materials move by diffusion.
    1. Particle movement from higher to lower concentrations
    2. Movement of water through membrane (osmosis)
  B. Some transport requires energy.
    1. Active transport
    2. Examples of active transport

Correct Outline Form
Include a title.

Arrange key ideas, subpoints, and details as shown.

Indent the divisions of the outline as shown.

Use the same grammatical form for items of the same rank. For example, if A is a sentence, B must also be a sentence.

You must have at least two main ideas or subpoints. That is, every A must be followed by a B, and every 1 must be followed by a 2.

Concept Map

1. Write an important concept in a large oval.
2. Add details related to the concept in smaller ovals.
3. Write linking words on arrows that connect the ovals.

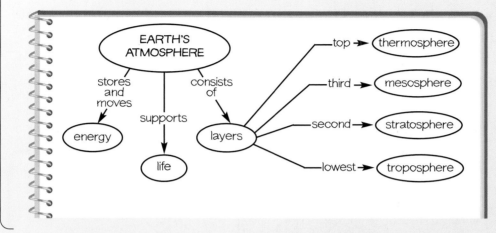

The main ideas or concepts can often be found in the blue headings. An example is "The atmosphere stores and moves energy." Use nouns from these concepts in the ovals, and use the verb or verbs on the lines.

Venn Diagram

1. Draw two overlapping circles, one for each item that you are comparing.
2. In the overlapping section, list the characteristics that are shared by both items.
3. In the outer sections, list the characteristics that are peculiar to each item.
4. Write a summary that describes the information in the Venn diagram.

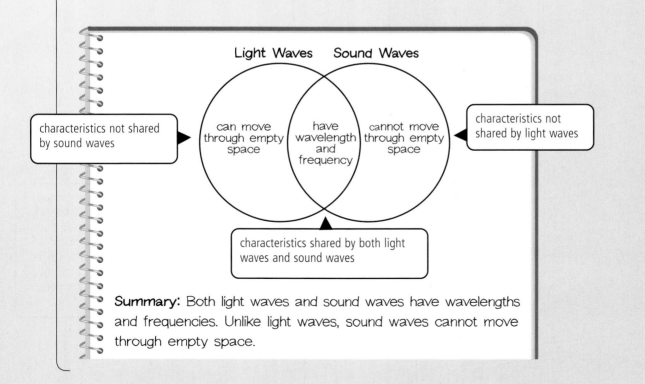

Summary: Both light waves and sound waves have wavelengths and frequencies. Unlike light waves, sound waves cannot move through empty space.

Vocabulary Strategies

Important terms are highlighted in this book. A definition of each term can be found in the sentence or paragraph where the term appears. You can also find definitions in the Glossary. Taking notes about vocabulary terms helps you understand and remember what you read.

Description Wheel

1. Write a term inside a circle.

2. Write words that describe the term on "spokes" attached to the circle.

When studying for a test with a friend, read the phrases on the spokes one at a time until your friend identifies the correct term.

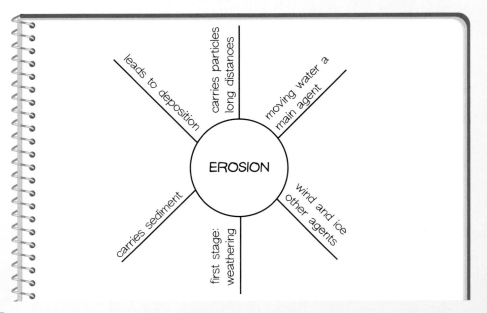

Four Square

1. Write a term in the center.

2. Write details in the four areas around the term.

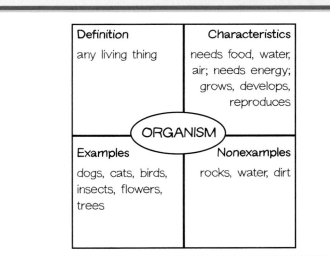

Include a definition, some characteristics, and examples. You may want to add a formula, a sketch, or examples of things that the term does *not* name.

Frame Game

1. Write a term in the center.
2. Frame the term with details.

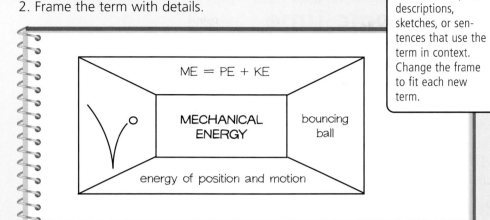

Include examples, descriptions, sketches, or sentences that use the term in context. Change the frame to fit each new term.

Magnet Word

1. Write a term on the magnet.
2. On the lines, add details related to the term.

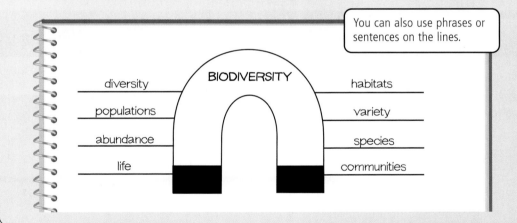

You can also use phrases or sentences on the lines.

Word Triangle

1. Write a term and its definition in the bottom section.
2. In the middle section, write a sentence in which the term is used correctly.
3. In the top section, draw a small picture to illustrate the term.

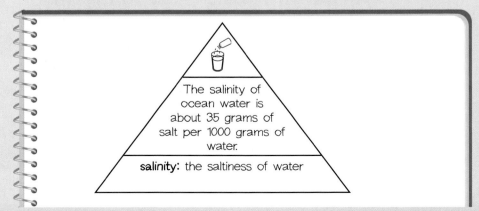

Appendix

Divisions of Geologic Time

The geologic time scale is divided into eons, eras, periods, epochs (ehp-uhks), and ages. Unlike divisions of time such as days or minutes, the divisions of the geologic time scale have no exact fixed lengths. Instead, they are based on changes or events recorded in rocks and fossils.

Eon The largest unit of time is an eon. Earth's 4.6-billion-year history is divided into four eons.

The Hadean, Archean, and Proterozoic eons together are called Precambrian time and make up almost 90 percent of Earth's history.

Geologic Time Scale

This geologic time scale shows the longest divisions of Earth's history: eons, eras, and periods.

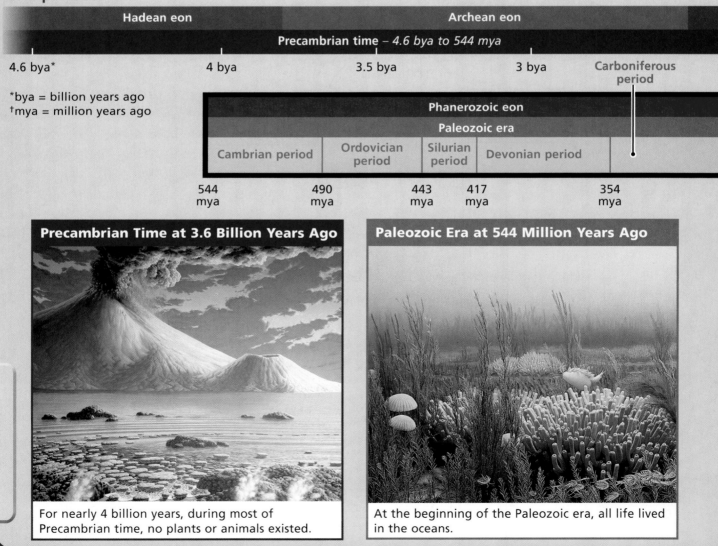

Hadean eon		Archean eon	

Precambrian time – *4.6 bya to 544 mya*

4.6 bya*   4 bya   3.5 bya   3 bya   Carboniferous period

*bya = billion years ago
†mya = million years ago

Phanerozoic eon				
Paleozoic era				
Cambrian period	Ordovician period	Silurian period	Devonian period	

544 mya   490 mya   443 mya   417 mya   354 mya

Precambrian Time at 3.6 Billion Years Ago

For nearly 4 billion years, during most of Precambrian time, no plants or animals existed.

Paleozoic Era at 544 Million Years Ago

At the beginning of the Paleozoic era, all life lived in the oceans.

The fossil record for Precambrian time consists mostly of tiny organisms that cannot be seen without a microscope. Other early forms of life had soft bodies that rarely formed into fossils.

The Phanerozoic eon stretches from the end of Precambrian time to the present. Because so many more changes are recorded in the fossil record of this eon, it is further divided into smaller units of time called eras, periods, epochs, and ages.

The Phanerozoic eon is divided into three eras: the Paleozoic, the Mesozoic, and the Cenozoic. Each era is subdivided into a number of periods. The periods of the Cenozoic, the most recent era, are further divided into epochs, which are in turn further divided into ages. The smaller time divisions relate to how long certain conditions and life forms on Earth lasted and how quickly they changed or became extinct.

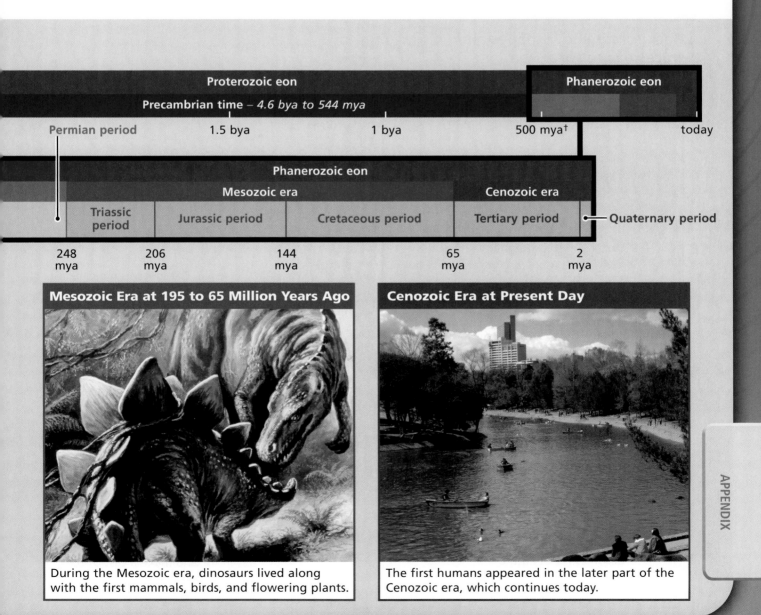

During the Mesozoic era, dinosaurs lived along with the first mammals, birds, and flowering plants.

The first humans appeared in the later part of the Cenozoic era, which continues today.

Fossils in Rocks

If an organism is covered by or buried in sediment, it may become a fossil as the sediments become rock. Many rock fossils are actual body parts, such as bones or teeth, that were buried in sediment and then replaced by minerals and turned to stone. Fossils in rock include molds and casts, petrified wood, carbon films, and trace fossils.

1. **Molds and Casts** Some fossils that form in sedimentary rock are mold fossils. A mold is a visible shape that was left after an animal or plant was buried in sediment and then decayed away. In some cases, a hollow mold later becomes filled with minerals, producing a cast fossil. The cast fossil is a solid model in the shape of the organism. If you think of the mold as a shoeprint, the cast would be what would result if sand filled the print and hardened into stone.

Fossils in Rocks

Rock fossils show shapes and traces of past life.

1 Molds and Casts

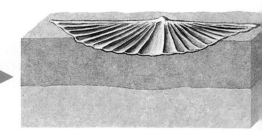

An organism dies and falls into soft sediment.

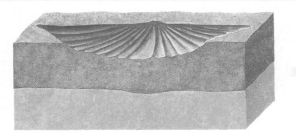

Over time, the sediment becomes rock and the organism decays, leaving a mold.

Minerals fill the mold and make a cast of the organism.

APPENDIX

2 Petrified Wood The stone fossil of a tree is called petrified wood. In certain conditions, a fallen tree can become covered with sediments. Over time, water passes through the sediments and into the tree's cells. Minerals that are carried in the water take the place of the cells, producing a stone likeness of the tree.

In this close-up, you can see the minerals that replaced the wood, forming petrified wood.

3 Carbon Films Carbon is an element that is found in every living thing. Sometimes when a dead plant or animal decays, its carbon is left behind as a visible layer. This image is called a carbon film. Carbon films can show details of soft parts of animals and plants that are rarely seen in other fossils.

This carbon film of a moth is about 10 million years old. Carbon films are especially useful because they can show details of the soft parts of organisms.

4 Trace Fossils Do you want to know how fast a dinosaur could run? Trace fossils might be able to tell you. These are not parts of an animal or impressions of it, but rather evidence of an animal's presence in a given location. Trace fossils include preserved footprints, trails, animal holes, and even feces. By comparing these clues with what is known about modern animals, scientists can learn how prehistoric animals may have lived, what they ate, and how they behaved.

A trace fossil, such as this footprint of a dinosaur in rock, can provide important information about where an animal lived and how it walked and ran.

Half-Life

Over time, a radioactive element breaks down at a constant rate into another form.

The rate of change of a radioactive element is measured in half-lives. A half-life is the length of time it takes for half of the atoms in a sample of a radioactive element to change from an unstable form into another form. Different elements have different half-lives, ranging from fractions of a second to billions of years.

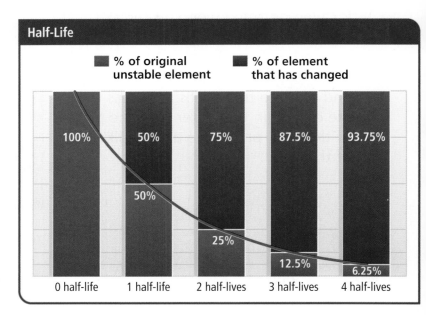

Half-Life

- % of original unstable element
- % of element that has changed

| 100% | 50% | 75% | 87.5% | 93.75% |
| 50% | 25% | 12.5% | 6.25% |

0 half-life · 1 half-life · 2 half-lives · 3 half-lives · 4 half-lives

Radiometric Dating

Radiometric dating works best with igneous rocks. Sedimentary rocks are formed from material that came from other rocks. For this reason, any measurements would show when the original rocks were formed, not when the sedimentary rock itself formed.

Elements with half-lives of millions to billions of years are used to date rocks.

Radioactive Breakdown and Dating Rock Layers

Igneous rocks contain radioactive elements that break down over time. This breakdown can be used to tell the ages of the rocks.

① **1408 Million Years Ago**

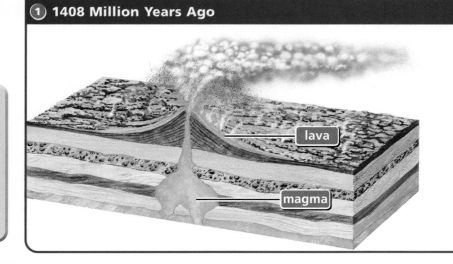

lava

magma

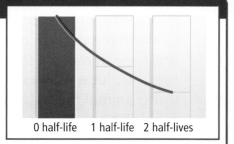

0 half-life · 1 half-life · 2 half-lives

When magma first hardens into rock, it contains some uranium 235 and no lead 207.

Uranium 235, an unstable element found in some igneous rocks, has a half-life of 704 million years. Over time, uranium 235 breaks down into lead 207.

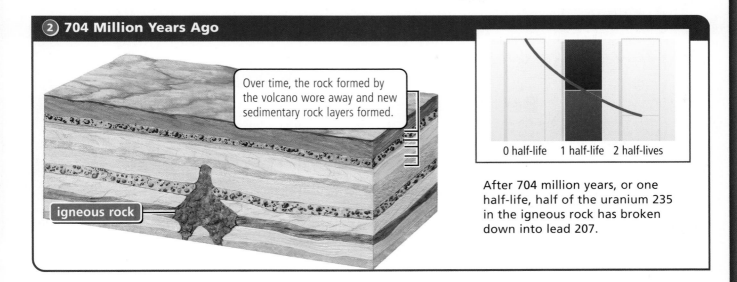

② 704 Million Years Ago

Over time, the rock formed by the volcano wore away and new sedimentary rock layers formed.

igneous rock

0 half-life   1 half-life   2 half-lives

After 704 million years, or one half-life, half of the uranium 235 in the igneous rock has broken down into lead 207.

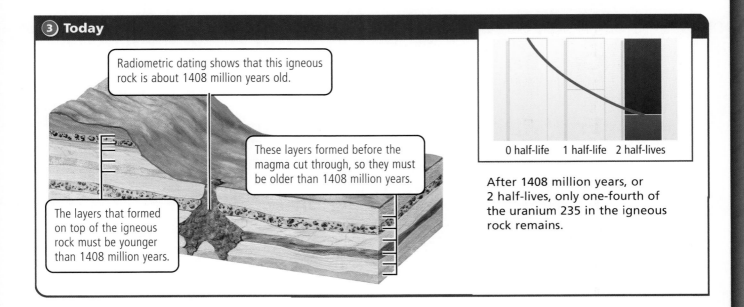

③ Today

Radiometric dating shows that this igneous rock is about 1408 million years old.

These layers formed before the magma cut through, so they must be older than 1408 million years.

The layers that formed on top of the igneous rock must be younger than 1408 million years.

0 half-life   1 half-life   2 half-lives

After 1408 million years, or 2 half-lives, only one-fourth of the uranium 235 in the igneous rock remains.

Just as uranium 235 can be used to date igneous rocks, carbon 14 can be used to find the ages of the remains of some things that were once alive. Carbon 14 is an unstable form of carbon, an element found in all living things. Carbon 14 has a half-life of 5730 years. It is useful for dating objects between about 100 and 70,000 years old, such as the wood from an ancient tool or the remains of an animal from the Ice Age.

The Periodic Table of the Elements

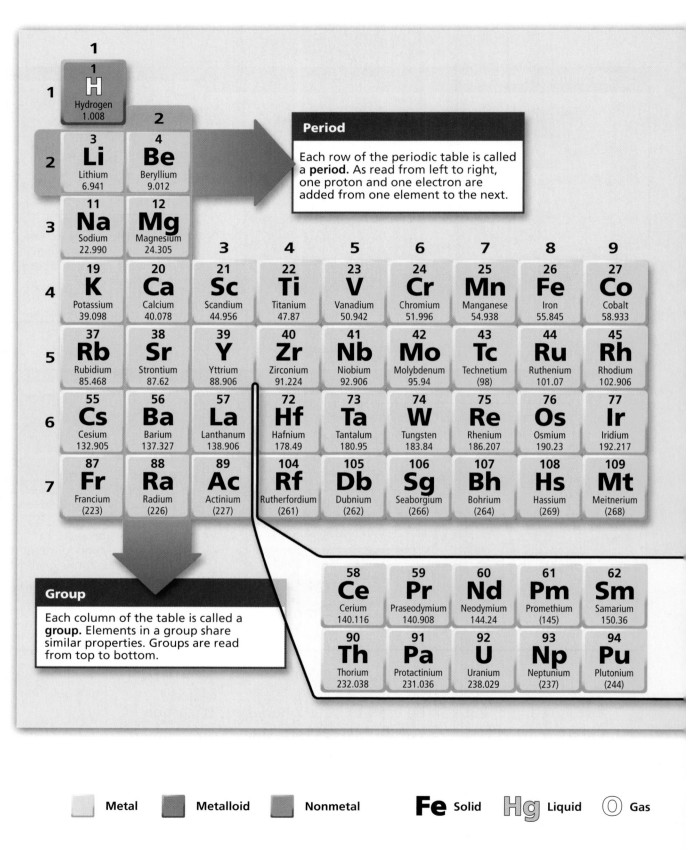

Period

Each row of the periodic table is called a **period.** As read from left to right, one proton and one electron are added from one element to the next.

Group

Each column of the table is called a **group.** Elements in a group share similar properties. Groups are read from top to bottom.

1								
1								
1 **H** Hydrogen 1.008	**2**							
3 **Li** Lithium 6.941	**4** **Be** Beryllium 9.012							
11 **Na** Sodium 22.990	**12** **Mg** Magnesium 24.305	**3**	**4**	**5**	**6**	**7**	**8**	**9**
19 **K** Potassium 39.098	**20** **Ca** Calcium 40.078	**21** **Sc** Scandium 44.956	**22** **Ti** Titanium 47.87	**23** **V** Vanadium 50.942	**24** **Cr** Chromium 51.996	**25** **Mn** Manganese 54.938	**26** **Fe** Iron 55.845	**27** **Co** Cobalt 58.933
37 **Rb** Rubidium 85.468	**38** **Sr** Strontium 87.62	**39** **Y** Yttrium 88.906	**40** **Zr** Zirconium 91.224	**41** **Nb** Niobium 92.906	**42** **Mo** Molybdenum 95.94	**43** **Tc** Technetium (98)	**44** **Ru** Ruthenium 101.07	**45** **Rh** Rhodium 102.906
55 **Cs** Cesium 132.905	**56** **Ba** Barium 137.327	**57** **La** Lanthanum 138.906	**72** **Hf** Hafnium 178.49	**73** **Ta** Tantalum 180.95	**74** **W** Tungsten 183.84	**75** **Re** Rhenium 186.207	**76** **Os** Osmium 190.23	**77** **Ir** Iridium 192.217
87 **Fr** Francium (223)	**88** **Ra** Radium (226)	**89** **Ac** Actinium (227)	**104** **Rf** Rutherfordium (261)	**105** **Db** Dubnium (262)	**106** **Sg** Seaborgium (266)	**107** **Bh** Bohrium (264)	**108** **Hs** Hassium (269)	**109** **Mt** Meitnerium (268)

58 **Ce** Cerium 140.116	59 **Pr** Praseodymium 140.908	60 **Nd** Neodymium 144.24	61 **Pm** Promethium (145)	62 **Sm** Samarium 150.36
90 **Th** Thorium 232.038	91 **Pa** Protactinium 231.036	92 **U** Uranium 238.029	93 **Np** Neptunium (237)	94 **Pu** Plutonium (244)

◻ Metal ◼ Metalloid ◼ Nonmetal **Fe** Solid **Hg** Liquid ◯ Gas

APPENDIX

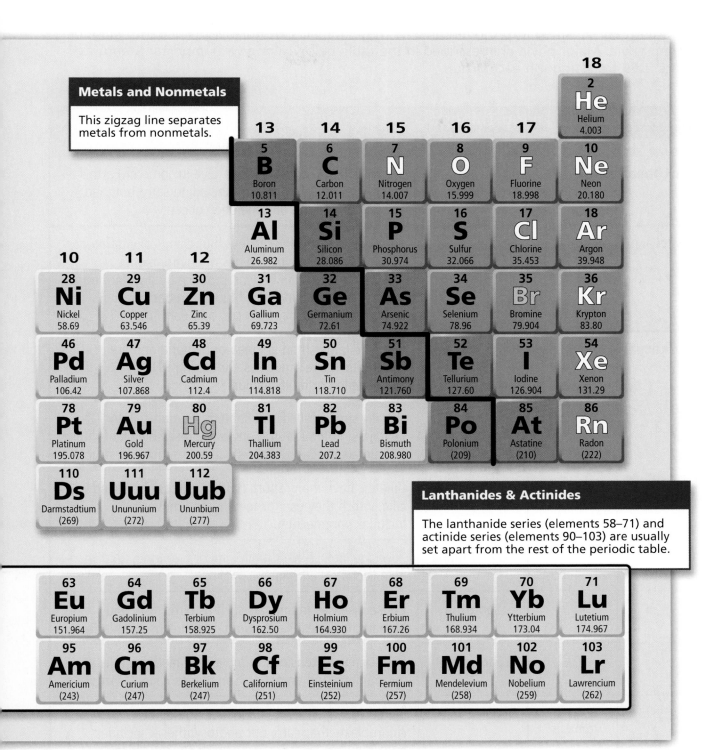

Metals and Nonmetals

This zigzag line separates metals from nonmetals.

			13	14	15	16	17	18
								2 **He** Helium 4.003
			5 **B** Boron 10.811	6 **C** Carbon 12.011	7 **N** Nitrogen 14.007	8 **O** Oxygen 15.999	9 **F** Fluorine 18.998	10 **Ne** Neon 20.180
10	11	12	13 **Al** Aluminum 26.982	14 **Si** Silicon 28.086	15 **P** Phosphorus 30.974	16 **S** Sulfur 32.066	17 **Cl** Chlorine 35.453	18 **Ar** Argon 39.948
28 **Ni** Nickel 58.69	29 **Cu** Copper 63.546	30 **Zn** Zinc 65.39	31 **Ga** Gallium 69.723	32 **Ge** Germanium 72.61	33 **As** Arsenic 74.922	34 **Se** Selenium 78.96	35 **Br** Bromine 79.904	36 **Kr** Krypton 83.80
46 **Pd** Palladium 106.42	47 **Ag** Silver 107.868	48 **Cd** Cadmium 112.4	49 **In** Indium 114.818	50 **Sn** Tin 118.710	51 **Sb** Antimony 121.760	52 **Te** Tellurium 127.60	53 **I** Iodine 126.904	54 **Xe** Xenon 131.29
78 **Pt** Platinum 195.078	79 **Au** Gold 196.967	80 **Hg** Mercury 200.59	81 **Tl** Thallium 204.383	82 **Pb** Lead 207.2	83 **Bi** Bismuth 208.980	84 **Po** Polonium (209)	85 **At** Astatine (210)	86 **Rn** Radon (222)
110 **Ds** Darmstadtium (269)	111 **Uuu** Unununium (272)	112 **Uub** Ununbium (277)						

Lanthanides & Actinides

The lanthanide series (elements 58–71) and actinide series (elements 90–103) are usually set apart from the rest of the periodic table.

63 **Eu** Europium 151.964	64 **Gd** Gadolinium 157.25	65 **Tb** Terbium 158.925	66 **Dy** Dysprosium 162.50	67 **Ho** Holmium 164.930	68 **Er** Erbium 167.26	69 **Tm** Thulium 168.934	70 **Yb** Ytterbium 173.04	71 **Lu** Lutetium 174.967
95 **Am** Americium (243)	96 **Cm** Curium (247)	97 **Bk** Berkelium (247)	98 **Cf** Californium (251)	99 **Es** Einsteinium (252)	100 **Fm** Fermium (257)	101 **Md** Mendelevium (258)	102 **No** Nobelium (259)	103 **Lr** Lawrencium (262)

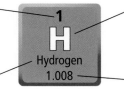

Atomic Number
number of protons in the nucleus of the element

1
H
Hydrogen
1.008

Symbol
Each element has a symbol. The symbol's color represents the element's state at room temperature.

Name

Atomic Mass
average mass of isotopes of this element

Classification of Living Things

Living things are classified into three domains. These domains are further divided into kingdoms, and then phyla. Major phyla are described in the table below, along with important features that are used to distinguish each group.

Classification of Living Things			
Domain	Kingdom	Phylum	Common Name and Description
Archaea	Archaea		Single-celled, with no nucleus. Live in some of Earth's most extreme environments, including salty, hot, and acid environments, and the deep ocean.
Bacteria	Bacteria		Single-celled, with no nucleus, but chemically different from Archaea. Live in all types of environments, including the human body; reproduce by dividing from one cell into two. Includes blue-green bacteria (cyanobacteria), *Streptococcus,* and *Bacillus.*
Eukarya			Cells are larger than archaea or bacteria and are eukaryotic (have a nucleus containing DNA). Single-celled or multicellular.
	Protista		Usually single-celled, but sometimes multicellular. DNA contained in a nucleus. Many phyla resemble plants, fungi, or animals but are usually smaller or simpler in structure.
	Animal-like protists	Ciliophora	Ciliates; have many short, hairlike extensions called cilia, which they use for feeding and movement. Includes paramecium.
		Zoomastigina	Zooflagellates; have usually one or two long, hairlike extensions called flagella.
		Sporozoa	Cause diseases in animals such as birds, fish, and humans. Includes *Plasmodium,* which causes malaria.
		Sarcodina	Use footlike extensions to move and feed. Includes foraminifers and amoebas. Sometimes called Rhizopoda.
	Plantlike protists	Euglenozoa	Single-celled, with one flagellum. Some have chloroplasts that carry out photosynthesis. Includes euglenas and *Trypanosoma,* which causes African sleeping sickness.
		Dinoflagellata	Dinoflagellates; usually single-celled; usually have chloroplasts and flagellum. In great numbers, some species can cause red tides along coastlines.

Classification of Living Things (cont.)

Domain	Kingdom	Phylum	Common Name and Description
		Chrysophyta	Yellow algae, golden-brown algae, and diatoms; single-celled; named for the yellow pigments in their chloroplasts (*chrysophyte*, in Greek, means "golden plant").
		Chlorophyceae	Green algae; have chloroplasts and are chemically similar to land plants. Unicellular or forms simple colonies of cells. Includes *Chlamydomonas*, *Ulva* (sea lettuce), and *Volvox*.
		Phaeophyta	Brown seaweed; contain a special brown pigment that gives these organisms their color. Multicellular, live mainly in salt water; includes kelp.
		Rhodophyta	Red algae; contain a red pigment that makes these organisms red, purple, or reddish-black. Multicellular, live in salt water.
	Funguslike protists	Acrasiomycota	Cellular slime molds; live partly as free-living single-celled organisms, then fuse together to form a many-celled mass. Live in damp, nutrient-rich environments; decomposers.
		Myxomycota	Acellular slime molds; form large, slimy masses made of many nuclei but technically a single cell.
		Oomycota	Water molds and downy mildews; produce thin, cottonlike extensions called hyphae. Feed off of dead or decaying material, often in water.
	Fungi		Usually multicellular; eukaryotic; cells have a thick cell wall. Obtain nutrients through absorption; often function as decomposers.
		Chytridiomycota	Oldest and simplest fungi; usually aquatic (fresh water or brackish water); single-celled or multicellular.
		Basidiomycota	Multicellular; reproduce with a club-shaped structure that is commonly seen on forest floors. Includes mushrooms, puffballs, rusts, and smuts.
		Zygomycota	Mostly disease-causing molds; often parasitic.
		Ascomycota	Includes single-celled yeasts and multicellular sac fungi. Includes *Penicillium*.

Classification of Living Things (cont.)

Domain	Kingdom	Phylum	Common Name and Description
	Plantae	🌳	Multicellular and eukaryotic; make sugars using energy from sunlight. Cells have a thick cell wall of cellulose.
		Bryophyta	Mosses; small, grasslike plants that live in moist, cool environments. Includes sphagnum (peat) moss. Seedless, nonvascular plants.
		Hepatophyta	Liverworts; named for the liver-shaped structure of one part of the plant's life cycle. Live in moist environments. Seedless, nonvascular plants.
		Anthoceratophyta	Hornworts; named for the visible hornlike structures with which they reproduce. Live on forest floors and other moist, cool environments. Seedless, nonvascular plants.
		Psilotophyta	Simple plant, just two types. Includes whisk ferns found in tropical areas, a common greenhouse weed. Seedless, vascular plants.
		Lycophyta	Club mosses and quillworts; look like miniature pine trees; live in moist, wooded environments. Includes *Lycopodium* (ground pine). Seedless vascular plants.
		Sphenophyta	Plants with simple leaves, stems, and roots. Grow about a meter tall, usually in moist areas. Includes *Equisetum* (scouring rush). Seedless, vascular plants.
		Pterophyta	Ferns; fringed-leaf plants that grow in cool, wooded environments. Includes many species. Seedless, vascular plants.
		Cycadophyta	Cycads; slow-growing palmlike plants that grow in tropical environments. Reproduce with seeds.
		Ginkgophyta	Includes only one species: *Ginkgo biloba,* a tree that is often planted in urban environments. Reproduce with seeds in cones.
		Gnetophyta	Small group includes desert-dwelling and tropical species. Includes *Ephedra* (Mormon tea) and *Welwitschia,* which grows in African deserts. Reproduce with seeds.
		Coniferophyta	Conifers, including pines, spruces, firs, sequoias. Usually evergreen trees; tend to grow in cold, dry environments; reproduce with seeds produced in cones.

Classification of Living Things (cont.)

Domain	Kingdom	Phylum	Common Name and Description
		Anthophyta	Flowering plants; includes grasses and flowering trees and shrubs. Reproduce with seeds produced in flowers, becoming fruit.
	Animalia		Multicellular and eukaryotic; obtain energy by consuming food. Usually able to move around.
		Porifera	Sponges; spend most of their lives fixed to the ocean floor. Feed by filtering water (containing nutrients and small organisms) through their body.
		Cnidaria	Aquatic animals with a radial (spokelike) body shape; named for their stinging cells (cnidocytes). Includes jellyfish, hydras, sea anemones, and corals.
		Ctenophora	Comb jellies; named for the comblike rows of cilia (hairlike extensions) that are used for movement.
		Platyhelminthes	Flatworms; thin, flattened worms with simple tissues and sensory organs. Includes planaria and tapeworms, which cause diseases in humans and other hosts.
		Nematoda	Roundworms; small, round worms; many species are parasites, causing diseases in humans, such as trichinosis and elephantiasis.
		Annelida	Segmented worms; body is made of many similar segments. Includes earthworms, leeches, and many marine worms.
		Mollusca	Soft-bodied, aquatic animals that usually have an outer shell. Includes snails, mussels, clams, octopus, and squid.
		Arthropoda	Animals with an outer skeleton (exoskeleton) and jointed appendages (for example, legs or wings). Very large group that includes insects, spiders and ticks, centipedes, millipedes, and crustaceans.
		Echinodermata	Marine animals with a radial (spokelike) body shape. Includes feather stars, sea stars (starfish), sea urchins, sand dollars, and sea cucumbers.
		Chordata	Mostly vertebrates (animals with backbones) that share important stages of early development. Includes tunicates (sea squirts), fish, sharks, amphibians, reptiles, birds, and mammals.

Glossary

A

adaptation
A characteristic, a behavior, or any inherited trait that makes a species able to survive and reproduce in a particular environment. (p. 22)

    adaptación Una característica, un comportamiento o cualquier rasgo heredado que permite a una especie sobrevivir o reproducirse en un medio ambiente determinado.

ancestor
A distant or early form of an organism from which later forms descend. (p. 29)

    ancestro Una forma distante o temprana de un organismo a partir de la cual descienden formas posteriores.

Animalia (AN-uh-MAL-yuh)
Part of a classification system that divides all living things into six kingdoms. Kingdom Animalia includes multicellular organisms, from humans and lions to insects and microbes, that rely on food for energy. (p. 63)

    Animalia Parte de un sistema de clasificación que divide a todos los organismos vivos en seis reinos. El reino Animalia incluye a organismos multicelulares, desde humanos y leones hasta insectos y microbios, que dependen del alimento como fuente de energía.

Archaea (AHR-kee-uh)
Part of a classification system that divides all living things into six kingdoms. Kingdom Archaea includes microscopic single-celled organisms with a distinctive cell structure that allows them to live in extreme environments. (p. 63)

    Archaea Parte de un sistema de clasificación que divide a todos los organismos vivos en seis reinos. El reino Archaea incluye a organismos microscópicos de una sola célula con una estructura celular distintiva que les permite vivir en medios ambientes extremosos.

atom
The smallest particle of an element that has the chemical properties of that element.

    átomo La partícula más pequeña de un elemento que tiene las propiedades químicas de ese elemento.

B

Bacteria (bak-TIHR-ee-uh)
Part of a classification system that divides all living things into six kingdoms. Kingdom Bacteria includes microscopic single-celled organisms found in many environments. Bacteria can be associated with disease in other organisms. (p. 63)

    Bacteria Parte de un sistema de clasificación que divide a todos los organismos vivos en seis reinos. El reino Bacteria incluye a organismos microscópicos de una sola célula que se encuentran en muchos medios ambientes. Las bacterias pueden estar asociadas a enfermedades en otros organismos.

binomial nomenclature
(by-NOH-mee-uhl NOH-muhn-KLAY-chuhr)
The two-part naming system used to identify species. The first part of the name is the genus, and the second part of the name is the species. (p. 52)

    nomenclatura biológica El sistema de denominación de dos partes que se usa para identificar a las especies. La primera parte del nombre es el género y la segunda parte del nombre es la especie.

biodiversity
The number and variety of living things found on Earth or within an ecosystem. (p. xxi)

    biodiversidad La cantidad y variedad de organismos vivos que se encuentran en la Tierra o dentro de un ecosistema.

C

carrying capacity
The maximum size that a population can reach in an ecosystem. (p. 82)

    capacidad de carga El tamaño máximo que una población puede alcanzar en un ecosistema.

cell
The smallest unit that is able to perform the basic functions of life. (p. xv)

    célula La unidad más pequeña capaz de realizar las funciones básicas de la vida.

classification

The systematic grouping of different types of organisms by their shared characteristics. (p. 44)

clasificación La agrupación sistemática de diferentes tipos de organismos en base a las características que comparten.

competitor

A species characterized by a relatively longer life span, with relatively few offspring, when compared with an opportunist species. (p. 96)

competidor Una especie caracterizada por una vida relativamente larga, con relativamente pocas crías, en comparación con una especie oportunista.

compound

A substance made up of two or more different types of atoms bonded together.

compuesto Una sustancia formada por dos o más diferentes tipos de átomos enlazados.

cycle

n. A series of events or actions that repeat themselves regularly; a physical and/or chemical process in which one material continually changes locations and/or forms. Examples include the water cycle, the carbon cycle, and the rock cycle.

v. To move through a repeating series of events or actions.

ciclo Una serie de eventos o acciones que se repiten regularmente; un proceso físico y/o químico en el cual un material cambia continuamente de lugar y/o forma. Ejemplos: el ciclo del agua, el ciclo del carbono y el ciclo de las rocas.

D

data

Information gathered by observation or experimentation that can be used in calculating or reasoning. *Data* is a plural word; the singular is *datum*.

datos Información reunida mediante observación o experimentación y que se puede usar para calcular o para razonar.

density

A property of matter representing the mass per unit volume.

densidad Una propiedad de la materia que representa la masa por unidad de volumen.

dichotomous key (dy-KAHT-uh-muhs)

A series of questions, each with only two answers, that can be used to help identify an organism's genus and species. (p. 56)

clave dicotómica Una serie de preguntas, cada una con solo dos respuestas, que puede usarse para ayudar a identificar el género y especie de un organismo.

DNA

The genetic material found in all living cells that contains the information needed for an organism to grow, maintain itself, and reproduce. Deoxyribonucleic acid (dee-AHK-see-RY-boh-noo-KLEE-ihk).

ADN El material genético que se encuentra en todas las céulas vivas y que contiene la información necesaria para que un organismo crezca, se mantenga a sí mismo y se reproduzca. Ácido desoxiribunucleico.

domain

One of three divisions in a classification system based on different types of cells. The six kingdoms of living things are grouped into three domains: Archaea, Bacteria, and Eukarya. (p. 61)

dominio Una de las tres divisiones en un sistema de clasificación basado en los diferentes tipos de células. Los seis reinos de los organismos vivos esta agrupados en tres dominios: Archaea, Bacteria y Eukarya.

E

element

A substance that cannot be broken down into a simpler substance by ordinary chemical changes. An element consists of atoms of only one type.

elemento Una sustancia que no puede descomponerse en otra sustancia más simple por medio de cambios químicos normales. Un elemento consta de átomos de un solo tipo.

emigration

In population studies, the movement of individuals out of an ecosystem. (p. 91)

emigración En estudios poblacionales, el movimiento de individuos fuera de un ecosistema.

energy

The ability to do work or to cause a change. For example, the energy of a moving bowling ball knocks over pins; energy from food allows animals to move and to grow; and energy from the Sun heats Earth's surface and atmosphere, which causes air to move.

energía La capacidad para trabajar o causar un cambio. Por ejemplo, la energía de una bola de boliche en movimiento tumba los pinos; la energía proveniente de su alimento permite a los animales moverse y crecer; la energía del Sol calienta la superficie y la atmósfera de la Tierra, lo que ocasiona que el aire se mueva.

environment

Everything that surrounds a living thing. An environment is made up of both living and nonliving factors. (p. xix)

medio ambiente Todo lo que rodea a un organismo vivo. Un medio ambiente está compuesto de factores vivos y factores sin vida.

evolution

The process through which species change over time; can refer to the changes in a particular population or to the formation and extinction of species over the course of Earth's history. (p. 17)

evolución El proceso mediante el cual las especies cambian con el tiempo; puede referirse a cambios en una población en particular o a la formación y extinción de especies en el curso de la historia de la Tierra.

experiment

An organized procedure to study something under controlled conditions. (p. xxiv)

experimento Un procedimiento organizado para estudiar algo bajo condiciones controladas.

extinction

The permanent disappearance of a species. (p. xxi)

extinción La desaparición permanente de una especie.

F

fossil

The imprint or hardened remains of a plant or animal that lived long ago. (p. 9)

fósil La huella o los restos endurecidos de una planta o un animal que vivió hace mucho tiempo.

Fungi (FUHN-jy)

Part of a classification system that divides all living things into six kingdoms. Kingdom Fungi includes multicellular mushrooms and molds and single-celled yeasts. (p. 63)

Fungi Parte de un sistema de clasificación que divide a todos los organismos vivos en seis reinos. El reino Fungi incluye a los hongos multicelulares, a los mohos y a las levaduras unicelulares.

G

gene

The basic unit of heredity that consists of a segment of DNA on a chromosome. (p. 33)

gen La unidad básica de herencia que consiste en un segmento de ADN en un cromosoma.

genetic material

The nucleic acid DNA that is present in all living cells and contains the information needed for a cell's growth, maintenance, and reproduction.

material genético El ácido nucleico ADN, ue esta presente en todas las células vivas y que contiene la información necesaria para el crecimiento, el mantenimiento y la reproducción celular.

genus

The first part of a binomial name that groups together closely related species. The genus *Felis* includes all species of small cats. (p. 52)

género La primera parte de un nombre biológico que agrupa a especies muy relacionadas entre sí. El género Felis incluye a todas las especies de gatos pequeños.

H

hypothesis
A tentative explanation for an observation or phenomenon. A hypothesis is used to make testable predictions. (p. xxiv)

hipótesis Una explicación provisional de una observación o de un fenómeno. Una hipótesis se usa para hacer predicciones que se pueden probar.

I, J, K

immigration
In population studies, the movement of an organism into a range inhabited by individuals of the same species. (p. 91)

inmigración En estudios poblacionales, el movimiento de un organismo hacia un territorio habitado por individuos de la misma especie.

interaction
The condition of acting or having an influence upon something. Living things in an ecosystem interact with both the living and nonliving parts of their environment. (p. xix)

interacción La condición de actuar o influir sobre algo. Los organismos vivos en un ecosistema interactúan con las partes vivas y las partes sin vida de su medio ambiente.

L

law
In science, a rule or principle describing a physical relationship that always works in the same way under the same conditions. The law of conservation of energy is an example.

ley En las ciencias, una regla o un principio que describe una relación física que siempre funciona de la misma manera bajo las mismas condiciones. La ley de la conservación de la energía es un ejemplo.

limiting factor
A factor or condition that prevents the continuing growth of a population in an ecosystem. (p. 92)

factor limitante Un factor o una condición que impide el crecimiento continuo de una población en un ecosistema.

M

mass
A measure of how much matter an object is made of.

masa Una medida de la cantidad de materia de la que está compuesto un objeto.

mass extinction
One of several periods in Earth's history when large numbers of species became extinct at nearly the same time. (p. 14)

extinción masiva Uno de varios períodos en la historia de la Tierra cuando grandes números de especies se extinguieron casi al mismo tiempo.

matter
Anything that has mass and volume. Matter exists ordinarily as a solid, a liquid, or a gas.

materia Todo lo que tiene masa y volumen. Generalmente la materia existe como sólido, líquido o gas.

molecule
A group of atoms that are held together by covalent bonds so that they move as a single unit.

molécula Un grupo de átomos que están unidos mediante enlaces covalentes de tal manera que se mueven como una sola unidad.

multicellular organism
An organism that is made up of many cells. (p. 13)

organismo multicelular Un organismo compuesto de muchas células.

N

natural selection
The process through which members of a species that are best suited to their environment survive and reproduce at a higher rate than other members of the species. (p. 21)

selección natural El proceso mediante el cual los miembros de una especie que están mejor adecuados a su medio ambiente sobreviven y se reproducen a una tasa más alta que otros miembros de la especie.

O

opportunist

A species characterized by a relatively short life span, with relatively large quantities of offspring, as compared with a competitor species. (p. 95)

oportunista Una especie caracterizada por una vida relativamente corta, que produce relativamente grandes cantidades de crías, en comparación con una especie competidora.

organism

An individual living thing, made up of one or many cells, that is capable of growing and reproducing. (p. xv)

organismo Un individuo vivo, compuesto de una o muchas células, que es capaz de crecer y reproducirse.

P, Q, R

Plantae (PLAN-tee)

Part of a classification system that divides all living things into six kingdoms. Kingdom Plantae includes multicellular organisms, such as trees, grass, and moss, that are capable of photosynthesis, capturing energy from the Sun. (p. 63)

Plantae Parte de un sistema de clasificación que divide a todos los organismos vivos en seis reinos. El reino Plantae incluye a organismos multicelulares, como árboles, pasto y musgo, que son capaces de fotosintetizar, capturando la energía del Sol.

pollution

The release of harmful substances into the air, water, or land. (p. 104)

contaminación La descarga de sustancias nocivas al aire, alagua o a la tierra.

population density

A measure of the number of organisms that live in a given area; the population density of a city may be given as the number of people living in a square kilometer. (p. 85)

densidad de población Una medida de la cantidad de organismos que viven un área dada; la densidad de población de una ciudad puede expresarse como el número de personas que viven en un kilómetro cuadrado.

population dynamics

The study of the changes in the number of individuals in a population and the factors that affect those changes. (p. 81)

dinámica de población El estudio de los cambios en el número de individuos en una población y los factores que afectan a estos cambios.

population size

The number of individuals of the same species that live in a given area. (p. 84)

tamaño de la población El número de individuos de la misma especie que vive en un área determinada.

Protista (proh-TIHS-tuh)

Part of a classification system that divides all living things into six kingdoms. Kingdom Protista includes mostly single-celled organisms with cells similar to those of the Plantae, Animalia, and Fungi kingdoms. (p. 63)

Protista Parte de un sistema de clasificación que divide a todos los organismos vivos en seis reinos. El reino Protista incluye principalmente a organismos unicelulares con células parecidas a las de los reinos Plantae, Animalia y Fungi.

S

speciation

The evolution of a new species from an existing species. (p. 24)

especiación La evolución de una nueva especie a partir de una especie existente.

species

A group of living things that are so closely related that they can breed with one another and produce offspring that can breed as well. (p. xxi)

especie Un grupo de organismos que están tan estrechamente relacionados que pueden aparearse entre sí y producir crías que también pueden aparearse.

system

A group of objects or phenomena that interact. A system can be as simple as a rope, a pulley, and a mass. It also can be as complex as the interaction of energy and matter in the four parts of the Earth system.

sistema Un grupo de objetos o fenómenos que interactúan. Un sistema puede ser algo tan sencillo como una cuerda, una polea y una masa. También puede ser algo tan complejo como la interacción de la energía y la materia en las cuatro partes del sistema de la Tierra.

T

taxonomy
The science of classifying and naming organisms. (p. 44)

taxonomía La ciencia de clasificar y ponerle nombre a los organismos.

technology
The use of scientific knowledge to solve problems or engineer new products, tools, or processes.

tecnología El uso de conocimientos científicos para resolver problemas o para diseñar nuevos productos, herramientas o procesos.

theory
In science, a set of widely accepted explanations of observations and phenomena. A theory is a well-tested explanation that is consistent with all available evidence.

teoría En las ciencias, un conjunto de explicaciones de observaciones y fenómenos que es ampliamente aceptado. Una teoría es una explicación bien probada que es consecuente con la evidencia disponible.

trait
Any type of feature that can be used to tell two species apart, such as size or bone structure.

rasgo Cualquier característica que puede usarse para diferenciar a dos especies, como el tamaño o la estructura ósea.

U

unicellular organism
An organism that is made up of a single cell. (p. 12)

organismo unicelular Un organismo compuesto de una sola célula.

V, W, X, Y, Z

variable
Any factor that can change in a controlled experiment, observation, or model. (p. R30)

variable Cualquier factor que puede cambiar en un experimento controlado, en una observación o en un modelo.

vestigial organ (veh-STIHJ-ee-uhl)
A physical structure that was fully developed and functional in an earlier group of organisms but is reduced and unused in later species. (p. 30)

órgano vestigial Una estructura física que fue completamente desarrollada y funcional en un grupo anterior de organismos pero que está reducido y en desuso en especies posteriores.

volume
An amount of three-dimensional space, often used to describe the space that an object takes up.

volumen Una cantidad de espacio tridimensional; a menudo se usa este término para describir el espacio que ocupa un objeto.

Index

Page numbers for definitions are printed in **boldface** type.
Page numbers for illustrations, maps, and charts are printed in *italics*.

INDEX

species, 54, *54. See also* taxonomy
    and binomial nomenclature, 52–53
    and classification, 54
    development of, *24*, 24–25
    evolution of, 67
    and genus, 52–54
    introduced, 88, *88*, 103, *103*
    naming, 52, 53, *55*
stability, population, 81–83, *82*
stages of population growth, 81–83, *82, 83. See also* growth, population
Standardized Test Practice
    classification, 73
    common ancestors, 39
    population growth, 111
starlings, 88, *88*
Steller's jays, 48, *48*
structural evidence, for evolution, 30, *31*

T

tables. *See* data tables.
taxon, 46
taxonomy, **44,** 46–49, 60–67. *See also* classification
    compared to classification, 44
    development of, 60
    and DNA, 34
    and domains, **61,** *61*
    genetic evidence for, 48–49, *49*
    physical evidence for, 48, *48*
    and species evolution, 67
technology, xxvi–xxvii. *See also* DNA, genetic evidence.
    and fossils, 74, *74,* 76, *76,* 77
    and human population growth, 100, *100*
    PCR, 77
    radiometric dating, 10, 76, *76,* R56, *R56*
    sonar, 97, *97*
    telephones as example of changes in, 17, *17*
temperature, unit conversion, R21, *R21*
theory, scientific, 28–29
Timelines in Science
    fossils, 74–77
tortoises, Galápagos, 20
trace fossils, *R57*
traits, 46
    and DNA, 33–34
turtles, 54–56, *55*

U

unicellular organisms, **12**
uniform spacing, *86,* 86–87
uranium 235, R57

V

variables, **R30,** R31, R32
    controlling, R17
    dependent, **R30,** R31
    independent, **R30**
variation, 22, *23. See also* natural selection
vestigial organs, **30,** *31*
vocabulary strategies, R50–R51
    description wheel, R50, *R50*
    four square, R50, *R50*
    frame game, R51, *R51*
    magnet word, R51, *R51*
    word triangle, R51, *R51*
volume, **R3**

W, X

water
    and early organisms, 13–14
    as limiting factor, 94
    and human technology, 100, *100*
weather, 93
wet mount, making, R15, *R15*
wildfire, 93

Y

yeasts, 66, *66*

Z

zebra mussels, 103

Acknowledgments

Photography

Cover © Martin Siepman/Age Fotostock America Inc.; **i** © Martin Siepman/Age Fotostock America Inc.; **iii** Photograph of James Trefil by Evan Cantwell; Photograph of Rita Ann Calvo by Joseph Calvo; Photograph of Kenneth Cutler by Kenneth A. Cutler; Photograph of Douglas Carnine by McDougal Littell; Photograph of Linda Carnine by Amilcar Cifuentes; Photograph of Donald Steely by Marni Stamm; Photograph of Sam Miller by Samuel Miller; Photograph of Vicky Vachon by Redfern Photographics; **vi** *bottom* © Richard T. Nowitz/Corbis; **vii** © Burke/Triolo/Artville: Bugs and Insects; **ix** *top* Photograph by Ken O'Donoghue; *bottom* (both) Photographs by Frank Siteman; **xiv, xv** © Mark Hambin/Age Fotostock; **xvi, xvii** © Georgette Duowma/Taxi/Getty Images; **xviii, xix** © Ron Sanford/Corbis; **xx, xxi** © Nick Vedros & Assoc./Stone/Getty Images; **xxii** *left* © Michael Gadomski/Animals Animals; *right* © Shin Yoshino/Minden Pictures; **xxiii** © Laif Elleringmann/Aurora Photos; **xxiv** © Pascal Goetgheluck/Science Photo Library/Photo Researchers, Inc.; **xxv** *top left* © David Parker/Science Photo Library/Photo Researchers, Inc.; *top right* © James King-Holmes/Science Photo Library/Photo Researchers, Inc.; *bottom* Sinsheimer Labs/University of California, Santa Cruz; **xxvi, xxvii** *background* © Maximillian Stock/Photo Researchers, Inc.; **xxvi** Courtesy, John Lair, Jewish Hospital, University of Louisville; **xxvii** *top* © Brand X Pictures/Alamy; *center* Courtesy, AbioMed; **xxxii** © Chedd-Angier Production Company; **2, 3** *background* © Alfredo Maiquez/Lonely Planet Images; **3** *top left* © Donald Windsor; *bottom right* Reprinted with permission from "Timing the Radiations of Leaf Beetles: Hispines on Gingers from Latest Cretaceous to Recent" Peter Wilf and Conrad C. Labandeira, SCIENCE V. 289:291-294 (2000). © 2000 AAAS.; **4** *bottom* © The Chedd-Angier Production Company; *top* Courtesy, Earth Sciences and Image Analysis, NASA-Johnson Space Center; **5** © The Natural History Museum, London; **6, 7** © Richard T. Nowitz/Corbis; **10** *top* © Mark A. Schneider/Photo Researchers, Inc.; *center* © Sinclair Stammers/Photo Researchers, Inc.; *bottom* © Novosti/Science Photo Library/Photo Researchers, Inc.; **11** *bottom* © Field Museum/Photo Researchers, Inc.; **13** *top* © Ken M. Johns/Photo Researchers, Inc.; **14** *bottom* © Lynette Cook/Photo Researchers, Inc.; **15** *top right* © D. Van Ravenswaay/Photo Researchers, Inc.; *bottom right* © David Parker/Photo Researchers, Inc.; *top left* © D. Van Ravenswaay/Photo Researchers, Inc.; **16** *top* © Paddy Ryan/Animals Animals; *bottom* © Layne Kennedy/Corbis; **17** *left* © Corbis-Royalty Free; **18, 19** *background* © Ralph Lee Hopkins/Lonely Planet Images; *bottom* © The Natural History Museum, London; *top* © The Granger Collection, New York; **19** *top right* © Volker Steger/Photo Researchers, Inc.; *right* © Zig Leszczynski/Animals Animals; *left* © Theo Allots/Visuals Unlimited; **20** *bottom right, top left, top right* © Tui De Roy/Minden Pictures; *bottom left* © Richard I'Anson/Lonely Planet Images; *background* © Ralph Lee Hopkins/Lonely Planet Images; **21** *right* © Hans Reinhard/Bruce Coleman, Inc.; *center, left* © Larry Allan/Bruce Coleman, Inc.; **23** *top left* © Bruce Coleman, Inc.; *background* © Paul Souders/Accent Alaska; **24** *top* © Hans Reinhard/Bruce Coleman, Inc.; *bottom, center* © Jane Burton/Bruce Coleman, Inc.; **25** © John Winnie, Jr./DRK Photo; **26** *top* © Marian Bacon/Animals Animals; **28** © Ed Degginger/Color-Pic, Inc.; **29** © Mark A. Schneider/Photo Researchers, Inc.; **31** *background* © Corbis-Royalty Free; **32** *center, left* © Photodisc/Getty Images; *right* © Mark Smith/Photo Researchers, Inc.; **34** © Photodisc/Getty Images; **35** © Norbert Wu; **36** *bottom* © Mark A. Schneider/Photo Researchers, Inc.; *top* © Tui de Roy/Bruce Coleman, Inc.; **38** © Hans Reinhard/Bruce Coleman, Inc.; **40, 41** © Burke/Triolo/Artville: Bugs and Insects; **41** *top right* © Ed Block/Corbis; **43** *top* © Robert Pickett/Corbis; *bottom* © U.S. Fish & Wildlife Service; **44** *right* © David I. Roberts/Photo Researchers, Inc.; *left* © S.J. Krasemann/Photo Researchers, Inc.; **45** *center* © Renee Lynn/Photo Researchers, Inc.; *bottom left* © Tom McHugh/Photo Researchers. Inc.; *top right* © Len Rue, Jr./Bruce Coleman, Inc.; *bottom right* © Frans Lanting/Minden Pictures; **47** *right* © Bill Kamin/Visuals Unlimited; *bottom left* © Norbert Wu; *center, top left* © Dave Fleetham/Tom Stack & Associates; *background* © E.R. Degginger/Photo Researchers, Inc.; **48** *top* © D. Ditchburn/Visuals Unlimited; *bottom* © M.H. Sharp/Photo Researchers, Inc.; **49** *top right* © Tom Brakefield/Bruce Coleman, Inc.; *top left* © Fritz Polking/POLKI/Bruce Coleman, Inc.; *bottom left* © G.C. Kelley/Photo Researchers, Inc.; *bottom right* © Tom McHugh/Photo Researchers, Inc.; *background* © Corbis-Royalty Free; **50** © Mary Evans Picture Library; **51** *top* © Photodisc/Getty Images; **53** *left, right* © Judy White/GardenPhotos.com; *center* © Tom J. Ulrich; **54** *left* © Joe McDonald/Visuals Unlimited; *right* © Photodisc/Getty Images; **55** *right* © John Mitchell/Photo Researchers, Inc.; *background* © Visuals Unlimited; **57** *top right* © Robert Della-Piana/photolibrary/PictureQuest ; *background* © Photodisc/Getty Images; **58** From *A Field Guide To The Birds Of Eastern And Central North America,* Fifth Edition by Roger Tory Peterson. Text copyright © 2002 by Marital Trust B u/a Roger Tory Peterson and the Estate of Virginia Peterson. Reprinted by permission of Houghton Mifflin Company. All rights reserved.; **59** *background* © Link/Visuals Unlimited; *bottom* © George Bryce/Animals Animals; **60** © Ken Lucas/Visuals Unlimited; **61** *left* © CNRI/Photo Researchers, Inc.; *center* © Wolfgang Baumeister/Photo Researchers, Inc.; *right* © Biophoto Associates/Photo Researchers, Inc.; **62** *top to bottom* © Corbis-Royalty Free; © Sharna Balfour/Gallo Images/Corbis; © Eric Grave/Photo Researchers, Inc.; © Rico & Ruiz/Nature Picture Library; © Dr. Jeremy Burgess/Photo Researchers, Inc.; © Eye of Science/Photo Researchers, Inc.; *background* © Courtesy of

NASA/Corbis; **64** *center* © Jim Zuckerman/Corbis; *right* © Masa Ushioda/Bruce Coleman, Inc.; *left* © M. & C. Photography/Peter Arnold, Inc.; *top* © Ed Degginger/Earthscenes; **65** © Jeff Foott/Bruce Coleman, Inc.; **66** *right* © Mark Taylor, Warren Photographic/Bruce Coleman, Inc.; *bottom* © Dr. M. Rohde, GBF/Photo Researchers, Inc.; *left* © Cordelia Molloy/Photo Researchers, Inc.; **67** © Gary Gaugler/Visuals Unlimited; **68** © Corbis-Royalty Free; **70** © John Mitchell/Photo Researchers, Inc.; **74** *bottom right* © Visuals Unlimited; *bottom left, top right* The Natural History Museum Picture Library, London; **75** *top left* American Museum of Natural History Library; *bottom right* © O. Louis Mazzatenta/National Geographic Image Collection; *center* © Peter Scoones/Photo Researchers, Inc.; *top right* © Geoff Bryant/Photo Researchers, Inc.; **76** *top left* © Science/Visuals Unlimited; *top right* © Kevin O. Mooney/Odyssey/Chicago; *center right* © Ira Block/National Geographic Image Collection; *bottom left* © James King-Holmes/Photo Researchers, Inc.; **77** *top left* © John Reader/Science Photo Library; *bottom left* © David Parker/Photo Researchers, Inc.; **78, 79** *background* NASA; **81** © David M. Phillips/Photo Researchers, Inc.; **83** *left* © Photo Researchers, Inc.; *right* © Wayne Lynch/DRK Photo; **84** *right* © Darrell Gulin/DRK Photo; *left* © Thomas Wiewandt/Corbis; **85** *left* © Stephen J. Krasemann/DRK Photo; *right* © D. Cavagnaro/DRK Photo; **86** *center* © Visuals Unlimited; *right* © Judy White/GardenPhotos.com; *left* © Betty Press/Animals Animals; **87** © Jim Sulley/The Image Works; **88** © Anthony Mercieca/Photo Researchers, Inc.; **89** *left* © Rod Planck/Photo Researchers, Inc.; *right* © Michael Abbey/Photo Researchers, Inc.; **91** © OSF/N. Rosing/Animals Animals; **92** © Tom Brakefield/Corbis; **93** © Najlah Feanny/Corbis; **95** *right* © Martha Cooper/Peter Arnold, Inc.; *bottom* © Dennis Flaherty/Photo Researchers, Inc.; **96** © Stephen J. Krasemann/DRK Photo; **97** *left* © Ted Spiegel/Corbis; *top right* © Wesmar; **99** *bottom right* © Rob Crandall/The Image Works; *bottom left* © Grant Heilman/Grant Heilman Photography; *top right* © Ed Degginger/Color-Pic, Inc.; **100** *left* © Bob Daemmrich/The Image Works; *right* © Geri Engberg/The Image Works; **101** NASA; **103** *top* © Ray Coleman/Photo Researchers, Inc.; *bottom* © John Serrao/Photo Researchers, Inc.; **104** *top* © Donald Speckler/Animals Animals; *bottom* © Janis Burger/Bruce Coleman, Inc.; **105** © Jeff Greenberg/The Image Works; **106** © Gaetano/Corbis; **108** *center* © Najlah Feanny/Corbis; *bottom* © Bob Daemmrich/The Image Works; **110** © Photo Researchers, Inc.; **111** © Wayne Lynch/DRK Photo; **R28** © PhotoDisc/Getty Images; **R52** *left* Mural by Peter Sawyer © National Museum of Natural History, Smithsonian Institution, Washington, D.C.; *right* Exhibit Museum of Natural History, The University of Michigan, Ann Arbor, Michigan; **R53** *left* © Ludek Pesek/Photo Researchers, Inc.; *right* © Steve Vidler/SuperStock; **R54** *top left* © Dorling Kindersley; **R55** *top* © John Elk III; *center* © Kaj R. Svensson/Photo Researchers, Inc.; *bottom* © Franceso Muntada/Corbis.

Illustration and Maps

Richard Bonson/Wildlife Art Ltd. **12, 13, 36** *(top)*
Patrick Gnan/Deborah Wolfe LTD **55**
Ian Jackson/Wildlife Art Ltd. **31**
MapQuest.com, Inc. **18-19, 88, 99**
Laurie O'Keefe **29, 32, 36** *(bottom)*
Mick Posen/Wildlife Art Ltd. **23, 57, 72**
Precision Graphics **97**
Peter Scott/Wildlife Art Ltd. **20, 24, 36** *(center)*
Dan Stuckenschneider/Uhl Studios **R11-R19, R22, R32**